DREAM CHASERS

Pursue Your God-given Dream.

by

Stephen D. Owens

Publisher By:
Alpha Lending & Investments, LLC.
Email: Alphalender@yahoo.com.

CONTENTS

ACKNOWLEDGEMENTS

Special Thanks to:

Mt Calvary Baptist Church for listening and giving me feedback as we studied the life of Joseph as a congregation. You all are amazing.

My Family, Lisa (wife), Stephen Jr. (son), and Rasheed (son) for encouraging me to continue to pursue my passion for writing.

My editor, Rausienne Broome (a.k.a. Teko) for all of her help.

SPECIAL OFFERS

<u>FREE E-BOOK</u>
Sign up for the **Leading Well Newsletter** and receive a FREE Ebook – **Rescuing Ambition.** Go here: www.Bit.ly/LeadWellNewsletter.

<u>FREE Video coaching on being a Dream Chaser with Stephen Owens :</u>
Sign up to receive three FREE video coaching sessions with Stephen Owens. These sessions will take you deeper into the principles and coaching exercises within Dream Chasers. Do not miss this great opportunity to develop the needed skills to purse your God given dream.
Go here:
www.stephenowens.org/dreamchasersbook

FOREWORD

You and I were born dream chasers.

Whether it was running through the kitchen with a dishtowel draped from your shoulders, bolting into the backyard to round up the bad guys with your superpowers; or if it was singing your heart out into a hairbrush while locking eyes with that diva in the mirror attached to your bedroom dresser. We were all born dream chasers until we experienced a few of life's disappointments, some 'less than positive' people, or just fell flat knocking the wind out of our sails, the smile off of our face, and the dream out of our heart.

Stephen Owens is a leader, pastor, and teacher who is trying to help us find restoration. To become once again what God intended us to be; a dreamer of His dreams. Seeing what isn't, yet working to turn it into reality.

I first met Stephen at a leadership conference where I was a keynote speaker in a room of nearly 1500 of the Midwest's best and brightest. After I spoke, Stephen approached me and said he'd love for me to come his way and speak on leadership in his part of the world.

To be honest, he was one of 5 who had made the same sort of request that day. I said yes to him, and yes to all of them.

Why was I so willing to say yes? Not because I had so much extra time, but because I have played this game many times and here is what I know:

• They are excited today, but they'll forget about this before they get home.
• They think it's a good idea now, but when they start planning they will see how much work it will take and they'll drop it.
• It's what they want to do, but when they figure out how much it costs... they'll want to do something else.

So, saying 'yes' to a conference attendee is not that big of a risk, because those are usually just wishful thoughts at the moment.

A few weeks later, I was standing in line to board a plane, ticket in hand, and conference schedule in my inbox. Stephen was not your average dreamer. That week I saw his leadership abilities. I felt his pastoral heart. I was impressed by his drive and vision. So, when he asked me to read an advance copy of Dream Chasers, it was a no-brainer.

There is no one better to write on the subject of having a God-given dream, realizing that dream, and taking ownership until God manifests that dream through you. This book will challenge you as it did me, to open wide your eyes to the possibility that we may have been plodding through life in a disinterested, disheartened, or possibly even defeated stupor. Yet, the opportunity for a full-on, in your face, change the world, leave no regrets life is at hand. Most importantly, this is no motivational seminar built on shoddy sociological experiments or thinly connected anecdotes. These directives are straight from God's word and are the application of truth.

The last night of the leadership conference to which Stephen had created and invited me, ended with a snowy evening and dinner out with him and several of his church leaders. We spent a few hours sharing, laughing and learning at that table. As I reflect on that conversation, I can see clearly the way Stephen had been leading that church. There were stories of dreams from the past, dreams in process and dreams yet to come! There were dream chasers all around him because he was leading as a dream chaser himself.

My prayer for you as you read this book is that you will plainly receive and clearly see the dream God has for you. That you would become a lifelong Dream Chaser!

More of Him, less of me

Andy Addis
Lead Pastor, CrossPoint Church
www.andyaddis.com

INTRODUCTION

"The LORD says, "I will guide you along the best pathway for your life. I will advise you and watch over you." – Psalm 32:8 (NLT)

God has given everyone a dream. No matter your age, gender, or ethnicity, God has placed a dream inside of you. The dream is not based on what you have experienced but on the future God has in store for you.

God has uniquely equipped you to go after the dream He has placed within you. The gifts and talents you have and will acquire will help move you towards the dream. Do not allow the difficulties of life to stop you from progressing forward. The problems you will encounter as you pursue your dream are there to build your strength and not hinder your progress.

This book will show you how to prepare for your dream. To receive the full benefit of Dream Chasers use it as a companion guide to the Bible. At the beginning of every chapter of Dream Chasers, a chapter(s) of the book of Genesis is referenced. Read the chapter(s) in the Bible first then read the chapter in Dream Chasers and complete the coaching exercise at the end of the chapter.

The coaching exercises will help you think through the information you will learn. Please, do not skip these exercises because they are designed to help you. This process will greatly enhance your understanding of the life of Joseph as well as how God can work through you to achieve your dream.

As you begin to read about the life of an amazing dreamer, I encourage you to think about the words of Harriet Tubman, "Every great dream begins with a dreamer. Always remember, you have within you the strength, the patience, and the passion to reach for the stars to change the world."(1) *You are the dreamer with the great dream. Now go after your dream.*

Index:
1.
www.brainyquote.com/quotes/quotes/h/harrie
ttub310306.html?src=t_dreams

Chapter One

Receiving a Dream in the Midst of Trouble.

~ Genesis 37 ~
"The pessimist sees difficulty in every opportunity.
The optimist sees the opportunity in every
difficulty."(1) - Winston Churchill -

The year is 1966 and a scrawny kid is being bullied by his classmates at Crittenden Middle School in California. This is the same year this 11-year-old boy goes home and tells his adopted parents if they do not transfer him to another school, he will stop attending school entirely. The family moved to the city of Los Altos, so he could attend Cupertino Junior High. While the bullying stopped, the boy still was not excited about school.

His adopted mom taught him how to read before he entered elementary school. Therefore, he felt bored at the idea of schooling. As a result, he became mischievous. It was not until the fourth grade that he began to show interest in school. His fourth grade teacher Imogene "Teddy" Hill often bribed him with candy and $5 so he could do his work. This teacher sparked a desire to learn in him and he skipped the fifth grade.

Who is the youngster? His name is Steven Paul

Jobs. Steve Jobs' childhood was not easy. He knew from an early age that he was adopted. He was born on February 24, 1955. His biological parents were Joanne Carole Schieble and Abdulfattah 'John' Jandali, a Muslim teaching assistant from Syria.

Steve was adopted by Paul and Clara Jobs who were a lower middle class couple in California. They did not have much money but they cared about Steve. Even when Steve changed schools because he was being bullied, the Jobs moved to another lower middle class area.

Steve did not have an exemplary childhood, but he did find out what he was interested in during this time. This is when he saw his first computer while he was enrolled in the Hewlett-Packard Explorer Club. He furthered his passion for computers by enrolling in electronic classes in high school.

It's a well-known story how as a teenager, Jobs called up William Hewlett, the president of Hewlett-Packard (HP) and asked for computer parts for a school project. From that conversation, William Hewlett was impressed with Steve, so he gave him the parts that he needed and offered him a summer internship at HP.

After high school, Steve enrolled at Reed College, which lasted for six months. Even though he continued to take classes in areas of his interest, he was not going to take the formal route to his career. This was a difficult time for Steve. He did not have much money; so to buy food, he would recycle empty coke bottles for money. He also had nowhere to live so he slept on his friends' floors.

During the mid-seventies, Steve was able to get a job at Atari where he primarily worked night shifts. It was during this time that his longtime friend Stephen Wozniak (Woz), developed a design for the first Apple computer. He showed the computer to Steve and he got excited. Steve and Woz raised $1,000.00 to build the computer. Steve sold his Volkswagen van and Woz sold his HP 65 calculator.

They initially wanted to sell the computer directly to consumers, which did not work well. Their first order came from a local computer store called Byte Shop. The store ordered 50 computers at $500.00 each, equaling $25,000.00. This was a massive order for Jobs and Woz but with the help of Steve's sister, Patti, and his friend Dan, they were able to complete the order.

This was the start of the computer giant we now know as Apple Computer. Yet who ever would have imagined that the young Steve Jobs who was adopted, bullied and bored in school would become the co-founder of a multi-billion dollar company? The story of Steve Jobs should help you understand, that no matter your childhood experience, you can still achieve greatness.

Possibilities

Dreams and achievement are not solely based on your childhood environment. God has the ability to give dreams to children that were born in paralyzing poverty. Yet in spite of their poor upbringing or background, they are able to make great strides in life.

I am sensing what seemed impossible has become possible. There are many people who have a dream, a vision from God, and because of what they have experienced, they feel as if their dream cannot come true. But, let me tell you, *"With God all thing are possible"* (Matthew 19:26).

It may not look like it's possible, but I'm encouraging you to *"walk by faith and not by sight"* (2 Corinthians 5:7). It may not feel like it's possible but you do not need to be moved by your feelings. You need to be moved by your faith in God.

This book was written to encourage you to go

after your dream. It does not matter what the dream is, as long as it honors God and God will receive the glory out of it. I encourage you to go after it. To help you get a better understanding of the process you will have to go through to reach your dream, we will examine the life of a man named Joseph.

The Beginning

Joseph's life is talked about in the book of Genesis in the Bible. You may be wondering, "Why should we study the life of Joseph?" Reason being, the life Joseph experienced rings true in the lives of most people whom I have been privileged to encourage on their dream.

Joseph's life helps us to understand this, the journey to our dreams is not a straight line or an easy process to go through. It's a journey of ups and downs, victories and losses, excitements and disappointments, and straight ways and detours. The life of Joseph is told in the scriptures through the lens of the providence of God. We see God working behind the scenes of Joseph's life to bring him to the fulfillment of his dream.

In the life of Joseph, there are no overt, direct interventions from God. There are no miracles mentioned. There are no new revelations of truth spoken by God through a prophet. The only intervention we find is the invisible hand of God working through bad circumstances.

Family Problems

The life of Joseph opens for us in Genesis chapter 37 in a place called Canaan. You may know this place by another name, Palestine. He is 17 years old and he is the second youngest of 12 boys. The scripture tells us he has sisters as well but we are not told how many.

Joseph was born into an extremely dysfunctional family. His father, Jacob had two wives and two concubines and all four women had children with Jacob. Yet, the woman Jacob loved the most was Joseph's mother Rachel.

Rachel had two sons with Jacob, Joseph and Benjamin, the youngest sons among the twelve boys. With this extreme family dynamic, there were bound to be some problems in the home. Yet, Jacob did not attempt to reduce the friction in the home, he added to it because of his poor parenting skills.

The Bible says, *"Israel (Jacob) loved Joseph more than all his children"* (v.3). Not only did he love Joseph the most, he showed the family that Joseph was his favorite. We are told that Jacob made Joseph a *"coat of many colors"* (v.3). The exact description of the coat is unknown. Jacob giving Joseph a garment such as this would be equivalent to a parent going to buy their children shoes and everyone receives $20.00 sneakers but one child receives shoes worth $150.00.

When Joseph's brothers saw how much Jacob loved Joseph, they began to hate Joseph. Their relationship deteriorated to where Joseph and his brothers could not have a decent and peaceful conversation. Moses, the author of the book of Genesis, wrote how Joseph's brothers "*could not speak peaceably to him*" (v.4).

In the midst of their family turmoil (favoritism, hatred and bad communication), Joseph had a dream that spoke to the greatness within him and what was awaiting him in the future. Please understand, no matter how bad your home life is or was, God can still give you a dream. He can give you an image of the future that can inspire you, and give you hope for the future.

What's the Dream?

Before we go into these verses, I have a couple of questions for you.

• What dream has God given you?
• What image constantly flashes in your mind about the future?

Whatever image consistently appears to you, you need to take it to God in prayer. Whatever you consistently think about, you need to pray about. That image maybe the dream God has given you to pursue.

In verses 5 – 11 of Genesis 37, we are told how Joseph was given his dream. To be accurate in these verses, Joseph was given two dreams. The first dream speaks of his brothers bowing to him.

Now Joseph had a dream, and he told it to his brothers; and they hated him even more. So he said to them, "*Please hear this dream which I have dreamed: There we were, binding sheaves in the field. Then behold, my sheaf arose and also stood upright; and indeed your sheaves stood all around and bowed down to my sheaf.*" (v.5-7)

The second dream speaks of his brothers and parents bowing to him.

Then he dreamed still another dream and told it to his brothers, and said, "*Look, I have dreamed another dream. And this time, the sun, the moon, and the eleven stars bowed down to me.*" (v.9)

While his brothers literally bowed before Joseph in Genesis 42, his parents did not. That's why you must pray about your dream, just because you can imagine it, does not mean it will come true. Nor does it mean it should happen.

To Tell or Not to Tell

While there are times when you should tell your dream to people, you must however be careful whom you tell your dream to. Joseph made the mistake of telling the wrong people his dream. He told his brothers and his father his dream.

When he told his brothers his dreams, *"they hated him even more for his dreams and for his words"* (v.8). His father rebuked him. Be careful who you tell your dream to. Everyone cannot handle the dream you have been given.

You may think everyone is going to be as excited as you about your dream but there will be some who will despise you for having a dream. Or they could be envious of you like Joseph's brothers did. Or they could be confused by it like Joseph's father was.

Instead of telling everyone your dream, do what Habakkuk 2:2 says, *"Write the vision and make it plain on tables."* Before you begin telling people your dream, you should write it down. When you write it down, make sure it is plain or in other words, make sure it's clear and vivid. Stop talking and begin writing.

When I was writing my first book, over 10 years ago, I made the mistake of telling people I wanted to be an author. I heard many negative reasons why I could not do it. As a result, I became discouraged and began to doubt my abilities. I heard very little encouragement to fuel my passion to write and be an author.

As I sit here to write my fourth book, I am glad I did not listen to them. Be careful whom you share your dreams with. They may not be an encourager; they may be a hater.

Trouble Erupts

Jacob and his sons were shepherds. One day, while Joseph's brothers were out feeding the flocks. Jacob told Joseph to go and check on his brothers and return so Jacob could know how they were doing. Here, we see Jacob's poor parenting skills pop up again.

Another reason why Joseph and his brothers did not have a good relationship was because Joseph would tell their father information about them. He would go back to their dad and give bad reports about his brothers. We do not know if the reports were true or false, but, we do know he used to say things about them.

Joseph was not innocent when it came the

sibling's relationship. Joseph was immature and childish, not because of his age but because of his behavior. His age was not the problem. There are immature people in every age group. Just because a person is an adult does not mean he/she is mature mentally, emotionally, or spiritually.

Read this carefully, immaturity will keep you away from your dream. If you receive your dream while you are immature, immaturity will cause you to lose your dream.

Joseph travels from Canaan to Dothan, about a four day journey, to find his brothers. As Joseph approached his brothers, they saw him from a long distance away. The Bible tells us *"they conspired against him to kill him"* (v.18). They began to plan on how to kill their little brother.

While Joseph approached, his brother called him "the dreamer." As they were talking about killing him, they made an interesting statement in verse 20, saying, *"We will see what will become of his dreams."* His brothers hated him because of their father's love, but they wanted to kill him because of his dream.

Some people mistakenly believe people reject them or are combative towards them because they do not like them, but more than likely it's bigger than you. Their rejection and frustration towards you is probably about your dream. The opposition you are receiving could be about your dream.

The devil (your enemy) does not want you to pursue the dream God has given you. If you reach your dream, people will be helped, people will be blessed, and the Lord will be glorified. It is not about you. It is about the dream.

The Pit

All of Joseph's older brothers wanted to kill him except his oldest brother, Reuben. He wanted to teach him a lesson, not murder him. He encouraged his brothers to throw Joseph in a pit instead of killing him. When God has given you a dream, he will use some of the most unlikely of people to help you.

When Joseph reached his brothers, they stripped off his coat of many colors and threw him in a pit. I hope you are able to see what they did. The coat represented favoritism and privilege. They removed their father's expression of favoritism and then threw him into a pit. Joseph has reached the lowest moment he has ever experienced.

This reminds me of the circumstances of life. Life has a way of stripping you of the stuff you think you need and cherish to show you the only one you ultimately need is God.

Even though Joseph hit the lowest point in his life so far, he still had his dreams. Some people think difficulties in life are signs that their dream will not come true but that's not the case. Hard times does not abort the dream, hard times is God's way of maturing the dreamer.

Being Sold

While Joseph was in the pit and his brothers were eating, a group of Medianite traders (another name for the traders were Ishmaelites) came by. Joseph's brother Judah had the idea to sell Joseph instead of killing him. Basically, why kill him, when we can sell him and make some money?

The Bible informs us that they sold him to the Medianite traders for 20 pieces of silver. That was the price of a slave. The Medianites purchased Joseph and took him to Egypt. When I think of what Joseph's brothers did to him, the word that comes to mind is betrayal. His brothers betrayed him. The people who should have been there for him sold him into slavery.

Have you ever been betrayed before? The people who should have been there for you abandoned you? The people who should have protected you, abused you? Those who should have covered you, left you exposed?

I would venture to say you have. If that is the case, I encourage you to forgive them. God has a way of using the betrayal of people to move you from relying on people to relying on God. One of the ways God uses the act of betrayal is for you to recognize that He is the one you must completely rely on and not people.

Besides, the only way some folks will move into Egypt (figuratively speaking), where the dream will come true, is because someone they trusted betrayed them or sold them out. Your dream is not going to come while you are living in Canaan, a place of comfort and favoritism. The dream God has given you will only happen in Egypt, a place that is unfamiliar and uncomfortable.

So in actuality, it was good that someone betrayed you. Because in their betrayal was the catalyst you needed to move to Egypt where you will have to depend on God so that your dream can be manifested.

The path that leads to your dream will lead you into unknown and uncomfortable territories. Places you have never been before, where you will have no privilege, no favoritism and sometimes no point of reference to lean on to. You will have to rely on God.

Deception

Back in Canaan, Joseph's brothers cooked up a plan to deceive their father. They killed a goat and dipped Joseph's coat in the blood and sent it to Jacob. As soon as Jacob saw the coat, he concluded Joseph was dead. Jacob sank into a deep depression and none of his children could comfort him.

At the end of chapter 37, we are given a glimmer of hope. Joseph was sold to a wealthy, influential man by the name of Potiphar in Egypt. Potiphar is an officer in Pharaoh's army and he is the captain of Pharaoh's guards. Even though Joseph is in slavery, he is alive. Since Joseph is alive, the dream is alive.

You may have gone through a lot in your past or you could be in a bad place currently. But, you should praise God because you are still alive. And as long as you are alive, then the dream is still alive. You still have hope for the future.

Think about Joseph, he was in a bad place, but he was still alive. Therefore, he still had a future to look forward to and so do you.

Points to remember:

1. The path to your dream is full of ups and downs

2. The dream is bigger than you.

3. As long as you're alive, the dream is alive.

Coaching Exercises

1. Write down your dream. Be clear and concise. Two to three sentences long.

_____

_____

_____

_____

_____

_____

_____

_____

2. Write down the areas you need to mature in. (Behavioral, emotionally, spiritually)

_____

_____

_____

_____

Here is some reading material to help you work through your growth:
• The 7 Habits of Highly Effective People – Stephen Covey
• Emotionally Healthy Spirituality – Peter Scazzero
• Experiencing God – Henry Blackaby & Claude King

3. Write down the names of the people who

betrayed you and whom you need to forgive. Ask God to give you the strength to forgive them.

_____

_____

_____

_____

_____

Index:

1.
www.brainyquote.com/quotes/quotes/w/winst
onchu156899.html

Chapter Two

Preparation for the Dream

~ Genesis 39 ~
"A dream doesn't become reality through magic; it
takes sweat, determination and hard work." (1)
- Colin Powell -

In 2009, she made history. Ursula Burns became the first African American woman to become the Chief Executive Officer (CEO) of a Fortune 500 company. Burns was named CEO of Xerox Corp.

Yet, she was not born with a silver spoon. If you were to look at her childhood and the environment she lived in, many would not have expected her to make history. Burns grew up very poor on the lower eastside of Manhattan, NY in a housing project in the 60's – 70's. Her childhood was similar to many inner city children who were raised in housing projects.

In February 2017, CNN quoted Burns in an article about the housing project where she was raised. She mentioned, "People would sleep under the stairs. You know drug addicts or bums … it smelled like urine out in the hallway. It was definitely not safe."(2)

Even though Burns was raised in poverty and in a difficult neighborhood, she had access to a good education at Cathedral High School in New York. Her education gave her a good academic foundation that prepared her for the work force. A door opened for her to become an intern at Xerox in 1980.

Burns internship led to a full time position at Xerox in the engineering department. She rose through the ranks of Xerox Corp to become CEO in 2009. Despite her many challenges, raised in poverty, being a minority in the US and in corporate America, Burns was able to reach what many people would call the dream job, CEO.

For many people, they believe individuals are the sole product of their environment. I do not believe that is the case. From my experience, people are the product of their decisions as it relates to their environment. As in Ursula Burns' case, her childhood environment could have been detrimental to her dreams; instead they became preparation for her future.

No matter the situations you have experienced, your dream can still happen. This chapter will allow us to see how Joseph was able to progress toward his dream in spite of the many difficulties he faced.

The Lord is With You

We found out from Genesis chapter 37 Joseph received his dream and as a result of sharing his dream, his brothers sold him into slavery. The life of Joseph is picked back up in Genesis chapter 39 where Joseph is a slave in Potiphar's house, in Egypt.

Even though Joseph is a slave, the Bible tells us, *"The Lord is with Joseph"* (v.2). His brothers may have forsaken him, but the Lord has not. Hey dreamer, as long as God does not forsake you, you will be all right. People may call you crazy and your dream stupid, it's okay. As long as God is with you, you have more than enough to pursue your dream.

Not only was the Lord with Joseph, he also became a successful man. Joseph was a man on the move. He was advancing in spite of his situation. Though he was a slave yet, he was breaking out of the position of being an ordinary slave.

There was something different about Joseph. He was not like everyone else in bondage. Verse three tells us what it was, *"The Lord was with him and that the Lord made all he did to prosper in his hand."* God was with Joseph and it was noticeable.

The scripture says, "*His master saw the Lord was with him*" (v.3). It was a noticeable distinction in how he lived and the way he worked. Dreamers, as followers of Jesus, there should be an obvious difference between you and your nonbelieving co-workers. People should notice a difference in your lifestyle and work ethic.

Joseph's work prospered. He got results. Joseph knew how to get things done. He was a productive individual. In order to get your dream fulfilled, you must be productive. Paul J. Meyer, founder of Success Motivation Institute, speaks to the importance of productivity when he said, "Productivity is never an accident. It is always the result of a commitment to excellence, intelligent planning, and focused effort."(3) Not only must you be productive, your productivity must help you arrive at positive results. Because people are watching you.

"What kind of people?" you may ask. People who are looking to hire and promote industrious people are watching. Individuals who are looking for results-oriented people are out there watching your every step.

Favor

We find out that "*Joseph found favor*" in Potiphar's sight. Potiphar was watching him. How did he find favor? Because he lived and worked differently than those who did the same job he did. And the scripture tells us Joseph was promoted.

Potiphar made Joseph "*overseer of his house and all that he had*" (v.4). Here is why, Joseph knew his God and he knew how to get things done. Dreamer, you have to know both. You must know your God and know how to get things done. Daniel 11:32 tells us, "*The people that do know their God shall be strong, and do exploits.*"(KJV)

If you want to advance towards your dream, you cannot separate your spiritual life from your work life. We see people doing it all the time, separating their spirituality from their productivity. There are some people who are super spiritual and unproductive. On the other end, there are people who are very productive but people do not know they are Christians.

As a follower of Jesus, people need to know both concerning you. By the way you live and speak, they should know that you believe in Jesus. And by the way you work, they should know you know how to get positive results. Proverbs 13:15 tells us, *"Good understanding produces favor"* (NASB). Joseph understood what he was doing, so he found favor in Potiphar's sight.

While Joseph was over Potiphar's affairs, the scripture says, *"The Lord blessed the Egyptian's house for Joseph's sake and the blessing of the Lord was on all that he had in the house and in the field"* (v.5).

Your Current Situation

Since you have been in your current position, can people say, "The team, the organization, the ministry or the business has been blessed?" Can they say, "Things are getting better or turning around since you joined them? In Joseph's case, Potiphar's house and his finances were improving.

This increased productivity motivated Potiphar to give Joseph more freedom and responsibility. Verse six says, *"He left all that he had in Joseph's hand."* Potiphar did not handle any of his affairs; he left them all to Joseph.

This is a concept every dreamer must learn, as they move towards their dream. **Learn to make the best out of your current situation.** Joseph was not in a dream job or in the ideal situation.

But, he was prospering. He was being blessed and promoted. Joseph was able to prosper in the midst of a terrible situation.

You may not like the situation you are in but what are you going to do while you are in it? You can learn a lot from your current situation. Ask yourself, what am I going to learn from this? What am I going to gain from this? What skills can I acquire from this?

Are you going to gain some knowledge and experience and grow up because of it? Or are you going to complain, murmur and make everybody else miserable when they work with you? I know it's not the dream, but it's preparing you for the dream.

Temptation

Verse six ends by describing Joseph. He was *"handsome in form and appearance."* Joseph had it going on. He had authority and influence, he was cute (handsome) and he knew how to dress (appearance).

With all that being said, the stage is set for temptation. Promotion always brings temptation. You may have heard the saying "new levels produces new devils."

In Joseph's case, the temptation came from his boss' wife. Potiphar's wife attempted to seduce him to have sex with her. Verse eight says, *"but he refused"*. Joseph said no. He was a man with standards. Joseph had ethics. There were certain things he would not do.

Listen to what Joseph told her in verses eight and nine, *"Look, my master does not know what is with me in the house, and he has committed all that he has to my hand. There is no one greater in the house than I, nor has he kept back anything from me but you, because you are his wife. How then can I do this great wickedness and sin against God?"*

I hope you see this, if you are going to make the most out of every situation, you must understand what Joseph understood.

1. Joseph knew his position in the house.

He knew the tremendous privilege and freedom and opportunity he was experiencing. You have to know what you have. *"His master didn't know what is with him."*

2. Joseph knew what he could do and what (or who) he could not do.

Potiphar kept nothing from Joseph except his wife. And rightfully so, she was off limits. We do not know if Potiphar told him that or he knew that instinctually. Whatever the case, Joseph knew she was out of his boundaries. Joseph knew his boundaries. You must know your boundaries in your current role.

Joseph said his master committed all to his hands. Which means, he trusted Joseph enough to promote him. Can you be trusted with promotion?

With more freedom and responsibility comes more temptation to touch things that are off limits. Before the Lord will promote you to your dream, He has to trust you with more freedom and responsibility. The way God knows He can trust you in order to promote you is how you handle your current temptations and situation.

God is More Important

Joseph makes a striking statement at the end of his conversation with Potiphar's wife. *"How then can I do this great wickedness and sin against God?"* (v. 9). This shows me that at the basis of his morality and ethics was his spirituality and holiness. He was being ethical for a reason. He did not want to *"sin against God."*

This also helps me understand that people are moral for a reason. People are not good just to be good. That's not enough motivation. You and I need a reason to say no to temptation. You need a bigger yes to God so you can say no to temptation. Joseph did not want to sin against God.

Even though Joseph refused her advances, she did not quit. One day, she caught him in the house by himself and she grabbed him by his coat and told him to have sex with her. He did not have a conversation with her this time; he run away and left his coat in her hands. I like the way one preacher summarized Joseph running away. He said, "He lost his coat but he kept his character."(4)

Potiphar's wife got angry and framed Joseph for a crime he did not commit. She accused him of trying to rape her. She told the servants that Joseph tried to rape her. Then she told Potiphar Joseph tried to rape her.

Falsely Imprisoned

The Bible says, when Potiphar heard the allegation, he got angry and threw Joseph in prison. Psalms 105:16 describes what happened to Joseph in prison. They *"put chains on his feet"* and *"iron around his neck."*

Wait, what just happened? Joseph did the right

thing and now he is being punished. He was fired and put in jail. Even though Joseph had morals, standards, ethics and holiness, he was put in jail anyway. Joseph was living right, working hard, and then he was accused of attempted rape and falsely imprisoned.

Where was God while all this was happening to Joseph? Verse 21 tells us, *"but the Lord was with Joseph."* In the midst of everything he was going through, God never left Joseph. You need to understand, as a follower of Jesus, God will never leave you, no matter what situation you find yourself in.

Joseph was not sheltered from trouble; he was sheltered in the midst of trouble. Potiphar could have killed him or had him killed. *"But the Lord was with Joseph and showed him mercy and he gave him favor in the sight of the keeper of the prison"* (v.21).

God gave Joseph favor with the warden. For some reason, the warden liked Joseph. It could not have been his work ethic or performance. He was in chains. I'll tell you what it was, God caused the warden to like Joseph.

Recognize Favor

One of the ways God shows His favor and blessing is by who He gives you favor and influence with. The favor of God is not only seen through material possessions, it's also seen as follows:

- When He causes people to want to be around you.
- When people want to help you.
- When people want to be there for you.

I encourage you to guard the favor and influence you have with people because it may be the favor of God.

We find out the warden *"committed to Joseph's hand all the prisoners who were in prison."* Joseph is elevated again. This time promotion comes while he is in prison. The same kind of freedom he was given in Potiphar's house he received in prison. Why? *"Because the Lord was with him and whatever he did, the Lord made it prosper"* (39:23).

Proverbs 12:2 fits this situation perfectly, *"A good man obtains favor from the Lord."* Joseph kept his holiness in the midst of temptation and God blessed him. He could be trusted with promotion.

Points to remember:

1. You need to know your God and your job.

2. Learn to make the best out of your current situation.

3. Every promotion produces its own temptation.

4. The favor of God can be seen through the favor of people.

Coaching Exercises

1. Do a 360 Review of your productivity. Rate your productive and work ethic. (Be honest with yourself.) Ask others to rate it as well. Ask your boss and/or leader. Also, ask someone who reports to you or follows you. (1 – very poor, 3 – average, 5 – very productive)

_____

2. What transferable skills can you learn in your current job (ministry) that will help you with your dream? Also, take some time to complete a Skills Assessment Test. There are numerous Job/Career assessment tools online to help you find clarity about your skills.

_____
_____
_____
_____
_____
_____

3. What areas of temptation must you be on guard for as you move towards your dream?

_____
_____
_____
_____

Index:

1.
www.brainyquote.com/quotes/quotes/c/colinp
owel385927.html

2.
www.money.cnn.com/2017/02/03/technology/
american-dream-ursula-burns/index.html

3.
www.brainyquote.com/quotes/quotes/p/paulj
meye393225.html

4. Warren Wiersbe Bible Commentary p.122

Chapter Three

Serving is the Solution

~ Genesis 40 ~
"The simple act of paying positive attention to people has a great deal to do with productivity." (1)
- Tom Peters -

In his groundbreaking book *The E-Myth*, the author Michael E. Gerber tells of an experience he encountered at a hotel in California called the Venetia. He was pleasantly surprised at the level of customer service at the hotel. The owner and management of the hotel cared about their customers' needs and experience, along with having the standard experience hotel guest care about, clean room, welcoming reception desk personnel, inviting lobby, etc.

The hotel training process taught the employees to ask their guest the brand of coffee they preferred as well as morning newspaper. They were to ask about the extra concerns that many hotels would not care about. The management made sure their customers knew they cared about their preferences. When the guest returned to the hotel, they would receive their brand of coffee and newspaper without the guest asking for them. Wow, what a great customer service!

Gerber's experience at the Venetia was so

memorable that he wrote about it in his book, which millions of people have read; thus, giving the hotel mass exposure and word of mouth recommendation. All because the owner and the management took serving their guest seriously. Great service opened the door to being promoted by Michael E. Gerber in *The E-Myth*, which is known as an underground bestseller. Do not underestimate the importance of serving people. Great service can change your life, your business and those you serve.

Connections

Chapter 40 opens and Joseph, the dreamer, is still in prison. He has been in Egypt for 11 years as a slave and a prisoner. He is now 28 years old and has not reached his dream. He has been through some ups and downs.

All while being in a place he doesn't want to be, he has been elevated and demoted. Even while he is in prison, Joseph is making the best out of his current situation. Besides that, he has two things on his side, God and he is alive. Therefore we are reminded, since Joseph is alive, the dream is alive.

Moses opens chapter 40 informing us about a scandal that happened in the political affairs of Egypt. Pharaoh (King of Egypt) threw his butler and baker into prison. We are not told what caused them to go to jail, except they "*offended their lord*" and "*Pharaoh was angry*" with them (40:1-2).

But, we find out that the same prison they were put in is the same prison Joseph was in. The scripture tells us, "*The captain of the guard charged Joseph with them, and he served them, so they were in custody for a while*" (v.4).

That's interesting; two high-ranking officials ended up in the same prison that Joseph was in. Now, Joseph was required to see to their needs. Some connections are divine connections.

God orchestrated that meeting. God set them up so Joseph's dream could come to life. We are told that Joseph served them while they were in prison. Joseph was a servant at heart.

Serving Others

Christians should be servants. Our hearts should desire to serve others. We have been called and chosen to serve God and people, in the church and outside of the church. No one should out-serve a believer. The Apostle Peter writes about this in his first epistle, "*As each one has received a gift, minister it to one another, as good stewards of the manifold grace of God*" (1 Peter 4:10).

We have the best model of servanthood, our Lord and Savior—Jesus the Christ who *"came not to be served but to serve, and to give his life as a ransom for many"* (Matthew 20:28). In church, at your job, in your neighborhood, your ability to serve others should be focused on excellence. Excellence is not about being perfect, it's about always attempting to get better.

The Bible tells us that the butler and baker both had a dream on the same night. They had different dreams with different meanings, but their dreams occurred on the same night. The morning after they received their dreams, Joseph went and checked on them.

Verse six says, he *"looked at them and saw that they were sad."* Joseph had taken the time to get to know these men so when he looked at them, he knew they were sad. He asked them, *"Why do you look so sad today?"* Joseph cared enough to ask them, "What is wrong?"

In order for you to develop a servant's heart, you have to care about people. It is here that we see Joseph has matured from being that immature 17-year-old young man with the coat of many colors. We know he has matured because mature people understand the importance of caring for and serving others. Joseph has grown up enough to know he has to care about people.

Opportunity

The butler and baker tells Joseph, *"We each have had a dream, and there is no interpreter of it"* (v.8). We have a problem and we do not have anyone to help us solve it. During this time, dream interpretation was a sought-after skill in Egypt.

One of the reasons Pharaoh kept magicians, sorcerers and wise men around was for them to attempt to interpret dreams. Joseph asked them, *"Do not interpretations belong to God?"* Basically, you have a problem and I know the problem solver, God. Joseph was telling them the one they needed to help them is God. Joseph asked the butler and baker to tell him their dreams.

Understand, peoples' problems are your opportunity to glorify God while you serve them. The first person to tell Joseph their dream was the butler.

The butler told Joseph, *"Behold, in my dream a vine was before me, and in the vine were three branches; it was as though it budded, its blossoms shot forth, and its clusters brought forth ripe grapes. Then Pharaoh's cup was in my hand; and I took the grapes and pressed them into Pharaoh's cup, and placed the cup in Pharaoh's hand"* (v.9-11).

Joseph interpreted his dream in verses 12-13.

Joseph replied, *"This is the interpretation of it: The three branches are three days. Now within three days Pharaoh will lift up your head and restore you to your place, and you will put Pharaoh's cup in his hand according to the former manner, when you were his butler."*

God used Joseph to solve the butler's problem. God gave Joseph a gift (ability), which was a sought-after skill so he could help someone in need. What skills has God given you that you are not using? People need what God has given you, but if you refuse to use them, you will be stopping your progress towards your dream.

Gifts & Skills

One of the major ways God uses to open the door to your dream is through the gifts and skills you have mastered. People are looking for people who have mastered a set of skills. What are your skills?

Your skills must be able to solve the problems people are facing. You will not reach your dream just because people like you. Liking you or having an affection for you is nice, but that will only help you get a conversation with them. It's your skills that motivate them to hire (pay) you and retain your services.

Proverbs 18:16 tells us, "*A man's gift make room for him, and bring him before great men.*" It's your gift, what you have to offer, your skills that make room for you. Your ability to serve people with your skills, to solve their problems, makes room for you.

Your gift will bring you before great men. Great men are people of influence who have a problem and need your skills, which you have developed and mastered. What are your skills?

Humility

Then Joseph goes out on a limb and takes a risk by asking for help in verses 14 and 15.

"*But remember me when it is well with you, and please show kindness to me; make mention of me to Pharaoh, and get me out of this house. For indeed I was stolen away from the land of the Hebrews; and also I have done nothing here that they should put me into the dungeon.*"

This is the first time we sense the feeling of frustration in Joseph. He wants out of his situation, so he asks for help and explains his situation. Now, a couple of commentaries have a negative view on Joseph asking for help.

But, as I see it, *"you do not have because you do not ask"* (James 4:2, ESV). Joseph's self-centered pride is gone and he has enough humility to ask for help. Some folks are so prideful that they will not ask for help. Now just because you ask does not mean you will receive what you are asking for, but that should not stop you from asking. Why? Because you do not know if you will be blessed with the help you need unless you ask.

With Joseph asking for the butler to tell Pharaoh about him shows us that Joseph knew the culture and laws of Egypt. During this time in Egypt's history, which is known as the Middle Kingdom period (2000 – 1775 B.C.), it did not have a sovereign ruler.

Egypt had a feudal form of government. While Pharaoh reigned as king, there were nobles and "nomarchs" (people who ruled over regions) in Egypt as well who had power. The nobles even held their own court proceedings.

In order to win over the people of Egypt, Pharaoh would speak of "ma'at" which is social justice (2). If someone believed they did not receive justice in noble court they could take the matter to the royal court to be tried. Therefore, with Joseph asking the baker to tell Pharaoh about him, he understood the process of law in Egypt.

When the baker heard the butler's good interpretation, he told Joseph his dream.

"When the chief baker saw that the interpretation was good, he said to Joseph, "I also was in my dream, and there were three white baskets on my head. In the uppermost basket were all kinds of baked goods for Pharaoh, and the birds ate them out of the basket on my head." (v. 16-17)

Joseph interpreted his dream as well.

So Joseph answered and said, *"This is the interpretation of it: The three baskets are three days. Within three days Pharaoh will lift off your head from you and hang you on a tree; and the birds will eat your flesh from you."* (v.18-19)

Scripture informs us, on the third day after Joseph interpreted their dreams, Pharaoh had a birthday party. He brought the butler's and the baker's case before his servants.

His Gift Works

Verse 21 says, *"Then he (Pharaoh) restored the chief butler"* and verse 22 declares, *"but he hanged the chief baker."* What Joseph said was true. He accurately interpreted their dream. His skill (gift) worked. Joseph the dreamer is also Joseph the interpreter. Joseph who has a dream is also Joseph who solves problems.

I am glad you have a dream. but can you help people solve their problem? The dream will become a reality when you learn how to help people solve their problems.

Joseph is a person who can solve problems. But, we have to remember how he found out they had problems. He was an observant servant who asked questions. Serving is the solution. Or rather, the solution comes when you become an observant person who asks questions while serving others.

In the midst of him serving, he cared enough to ask, "What is wrong?" Serving people with a caring heart in order to help solve problems will open the door to your dream. Here is a great quote from Pastor Robert Schuller,

"The secret of success is to find a need and fill it, to find a hurt and heal it, to find somebody with a problem and offer to help solve it."(3)

Your Skills

Here are four steps to help you become a problem solver.
1. Recognize the skills God has given you.
2. Develop those skills and master them.
3. Research what needs match your skills.
4. Then work on filling those needs with your skills.

No matter what field you are in or want to be in, these four action steps will help you move towards your dream.

Here is a bit of irony. Even though Joseph is in a dungeon and ready to be done with his situation, he should have a sense of hope because dreams come true. His dream has not come true yet. But he has just witnessed two dreams come to life.

Celebrate for Others

That's why you should get excited when you see those close to you reach their dreams because if their dream can come true, then your dream can come true too. God is not a respecter of people. If He has done it for one, He can do the same for you.

Do not be negative when people walk into their dream, congratulate them and celebrate their achievement. Celebrate them, because you may be the next one to take that walk. You need to celebrate God and thank Him for keeping His promises and fulfilling dreams.

We find out at the end of the chapter that the butler forgot Joseph. But God did not forget him. God was with Joseph when his brothers threw him in the pit. God was with him when he arrived at Potiphar's house. God was with him when he was promoted and when he was accused of attempted rape. God is with Joseph now even when the butler has forgotten about him.

Just because people may have forgotten you, does not mean God has forgotten you. As Hebrews 6:10 declares, *"For God is not unrighteous to forget your work and labor of love."* God will not forget you, no matter what situation you find yourself in.

Points to remember:
1. Some connections are divine connections.
2. Christians should have hearts to serve.
3. People's problems are your opportunities.

Coaching Exercises

1. Do a 360 Review of your customer service skills. Rate your level of service. (Be honest with yourself.) Ask others to rate it as well. Ask your boss and/or leader. Also, ask someone who reports to you or follows you. (1 – very poor, 3 – average, 5 – very productive)

_____

2. What skills do you have that will help you solve people's problems?

_____
_____
_____
_____
_____

3. What problems require your skills?

_____
_____
_____
_____

Index:

1. www.brainyquote.com/quotes/quotes/t/tompeters194017.html

2. Nelson's New Illustrated Bible Manners & Customs by Howard F. Vos. P. 48

3. www1.cbn.com/700club/dr-robert-schuller-legacy-power

Chapter Four

Their Need is Your Blessing

~ Genesis 41 ~
"Patience is the companion of wisdom." (1)
- Saint Augustine -

"Every time I go home, people keep asking me to bring stuff."(2) This is the statement Chris Folayan made when he discussed his amazing business Mall for Africa. Mr. Folayan created an online platform for consumers in Africa, starting in Nigeria, to purchase products from retailers in America and the United Kingdom.

Folayan was raised in Nigeria. He came to the United States to attend college and then began his career in corporate America. When he would travel back home, his family and friends in Nigeria would ask him to bring American products with him. Folayan noticed the frequency of the request for American products and he realized that he had tapped into a market that had a great demand for international products with very few suppliers.

US and UK brand retailers were not shipping their products to Nigeria. Folayan created a multi-functional business called Mall for Africa, to meet the need in Africa. It's for people who want to purchase foreign products. The business initially started in his spare bedroom and he created an online form for his family and friends to request products and make payments. When he would travel back to Nigeria, he would take the items with him and deliver the items to his customers.

When demand grew on the online form, he created a phone app. The app essentially did the same thing the online form did but it also had the capability to let the customer know how much the item costs. In 2011, he launched the website MallforAfrica.com. Over time, Folayan developed relationships with major brand name retailers from the US and UK to sell their products through Mall for Africa. He and his company also worked through the logistical difficulties of shipping the products to Africa and currency exchange rates for payments.

Today, Mall for Africa is a multi-continental business with over a couple of hundred US and UK retailers selling products to Africans. Africans can purchase products directly on MallforAfrica.com and the Mall for Africa will arrange shipping and converting the currencies into dollars so the retailers can receive payment. The Mall for Africa have local delivery pickup locations in Africa and warehouses in the US and UK. The Mall for Africa is doing business in America, the United Kingdom and Africa because Chris Folayan sought to fill a growing need in Africa. Their need became his blessing.

Patience

Genesis chapter 41 opens, informing us two years has passed and Joseph is still in prison. He is ready to get out, but without a visible way to exit his situation. All he can do is wait.

Have you ever been in a situation you could not change and all you could do is wait? You may be in a moment of waiting right now. Let me encourage you with Psalm 27:14 *"Wait patiently for the Lord. Be brave and courageous. Yes, wait patiently for the Lord"* (NLT).

Waiting is a part of the process to moving towards your dream. The timing has to be right for your dream to come to pass. The right timing is God's timing.

While Joseph is waiting and still serving, God is working. Understand, if you are in a situation that you cannot change, know this, God is working behind the scenes. Just because you do not see a change does not mean change is not coming. You continue to develop your skill, finding needs, solving problems and serving people and let God handle the rest.

Stephen D. Owens

Providence

We are told that Pharaoh has two dreams in the same night. While there is some discrepancy over the name of this Pharaoh, most Egyptologist point to Sesortris III to be the Pharaoh during this time.(3) The scriptures tell us about the dreams.

"Suddenly, there came up out of the river seven cows, fine looking and fat; and they fed in the meadow. Then behold, seven other cows came up after them out of the river, ugly and gaunt, and stood by the other cows on the bank of the river. And the ugly and gaunt cows ate up the seven fine looking and fat cows. So Pharaoh awoke. He slept and dreamed a second time; and suddenly seven heads of grain came up on one stalk, plump and good. Then behold, seven thin heads, blighted by the east wind, sprang up after them. And the seven thin heads devoured the seven plump and full heads. So Pharaoh awoke, and indeed, it was a dream." (v.2-7)

Verse eight says, when Pharaoh awoke after the second dream *"his spirit was troubled."* He called together his magicians and wise men and told them the dreams. Scripture tells us, *"but there was no one who could interpret them for pharaoh."* (v. 8)

Here is a powerful man; ruler of Egypt, with a problem and no one could solve it. It is at this moment, that the butler remembered Joseph; not because Joseph was a nice guy who helped him out when he was in need so now he was returning the favor. No. His boss had a need that no one could fill and he remembered a problem he had when no one could fill it. He remembered the person who had the skills to solve his problem. In verses 9 - 13, the butler told Pharaoh about how he met Joseph and how Joseph solved his problem.

The butler informed Pharaoh, "*I remember my faults this day. When Pharaoh was angry with his servants, and put me in custody in the house of the captain of the guard, both me and the chief baker, we each had a dream in one night, he and I. Each of us dreamed according to the interpretation of his own dream. Now there was a young Hebrew man with us there, a servant of the captain of the guard. And we told him, and he interpreted our dreams for us; to each man he interpreted according to his own dream. And it came to pass, just as he interpreted for us, so it happened. He restored me to my office, and he hanged him.*" (v. 9 – 13)

Every day you go to work (and church), you need to do your job to the best of your ability — serving people with excellence. You do not know who the person will be that could refer you to the biggest opportunity (promotion or contract) of your life. In Joseph's case, it turned out to be the butler. But in your case, you do not know whom

God will use.

Preparation

Verse 14 reads, *"Then Pharaoh sent and called Joseph, and they brought him quickly out of the dungeon; and he shaved, changed his clothing and came to Pharaoh."*

Joseph had been in bondage for 13 years and in a moment, his life changed forever. He hit a "defining moment" in his life; a moment that was pregnant with possibilities. Some would say, he entered into a "kairos moment." Kairos is a Greek word for timing. It means the right time or opportune moment. It's a moment that has been ordained by God.

In one day, his life changed, *"he is brought out quickly."* All the barriers that were keeping him in bondage were removed because the king of Egypt was calling for him. When God is ready to move you into your dream, no one will be able to stop you. When it is God's time, He will pull you out of the situation with no delay.

Let's look at what Joseph did when he came out of prison. The Bible tells us he prepared himself for his meeting with the king. You have to prepare yourself for opportunity.

He cleaned himself up. He shaved and changed his clothes. Shaving himself indicated he understood the culture he was walking into. Egyptians did not wear beards at that time. Joseph changing his clothes shows us he knew how to present himself in meetings.

Understand this, first impressions are crucial. Take time to read up on the dream God has given you.

1. How do they behave in that industry?
2. What is the culture like?
3. How do they dress?
4. What are the norms and traditions?

Solving a Major Problem

When Joseph arrived at the palace, Pharaoh told Joseph, *"I had a dream and no one can interpret it"* (v.15). This man of influence had a problem and no one could solve it. Pharaoh said, *"I have heard it said of you that you can understand a dream, to interpret it."* I heard you have the skills to solve my problem.

It is in this initial conversation we see why Pharaoh released Joseph out of prison. It was his skill (mastered gift). It was his ability to solve problems and to fill a need in the marketplace. Remember, people who know how to solve problems best handle opportunities.

If Joseph's name had come before Pharaoh earlier, the power dynamic would have been wrong. The king would have seen him as a prisoner who wanted mercy. But now, the king sees him as someone that has the potential to solve his problem and it just so happens he is in prison. Do not attempt to rush God, dreamer. The timing must be right for God to move you forward. You keep learning and developing your skills and solving problems where you are.

Joseph showed his dependence on God and not his ability, skills. He had confidence in God, not himself. He told Pharaoh, *"It is not in me; God will give Pharaoh an answer of peace."* Basically, I'm just a vessel; God is the real problem solver.

In verses 17 – 24, Pharaoh told Joseph his two dreams:

Pharaoh said, *"Behold, in my dream I stood on the bank of the river. Suddenly seven cows came up out of the river, fine looking and fat; and they fed in the meadow. Then behold, seven other cows came up after them, poor and very ugly and gaunt, such ugliness as I have never seen in all the land of Egypt. And the gaunt and ugly cows ate up the first seven, the fat cows. When they had eaten them up, no one would have known that they had eaten them, for they were just as ugly as at the beginning. So I awoke. Also I saw in my dream, and suddenly seven heads came up on one stalk, full and good. Then behold, seven heads, withered, thin, and blighted by the east wind, sprang up after them. And the thin heads devoured the seven good heads. So I told this to the magicians, but there was no one who could explain it to me."*

Joseph's response to Pharaoh is in verses 25 – 31,

Joseph said, *"The dreams of Pharaoh are one; God has shown Pharaoh what He is about to do: The seven good cows are seven years, and the seven good heads are seven years; the dreams are one. And the seven thin and ugly cows which came up after them are seven years, and the seven empty heads blighted by the east wind are seven years of famine. This is the thing which I have spoken to Pharaoh. God has shown Pharaoh what He is about to do. Indeed seven years of great plenty will come throughout all the land of Egypt; but after them seven years of famine will arise, and all the plenty will be forgotten in the land of Egypt; and the famine will deplete the land. So the plenty will not be known in the land because of the famine following, for it will be very severe. And the dream was repeated to Pharaoh twice because the thing is established by God, and God will shortly bring it to pass."*

Give a Solution

Joseph was able to tell Pharaoh what the dreams meant and who caused him to have the dreams. He diagnosed the problem and told him what (rather Who) caused it. You have to learn how to identify problems before you can solve them. People who do not know what they are doing, suggest solutions without first knowing what the problem is.

Professionals determine the problem, and then give solutions to fix the issue. Joseph was a professional. Not only was Joseph a professional, he was also courageous. He gave an unsolicited solution to Pharaoh's dilemma.

He advised Pharaoh to *"select a discerning and wise man and set him over the land of Egypt"* (v.33). Pharaoh, you need to find a leader. You need a point person to handle the situation. Then *"let him (the leader) appoint officers over the land to collect one fifth of the produce"* during the seven years of plenty. Pharaoh, let your leader pick his staff, build the team, so they can collect 20% of the grain when there is abundance. Then store the grain in the cities as a reserve for when the famine arrives.

I really appreciate the fact that Joseph knew what he was talking about. He told Pharaoh in so many words, you need a governmental division to deal with this economic problem the nation is facing and here is a plan (snapshot) on how to do it.

Let me encourage people that refuse to give free advice. You do not need to give away everything. But, for people to want to retain your services, they have to know what you can provide. If they never worked with you before, you need to let them experience a little of what you have to offer. That is why stores give away samples. The samples let you know that their product is the solution for your need.

Skill Set

Besides, if you have more than one tool in your tool belt, you will not mind showing folks how to handle one tool. Joseph had more than one tool in his belt. As a matter of fact, he had a belt and bag of tools. He had a tool set (skill sets).

Check out Joseph's skill sets.
- He identified problems.
- He solved problems.
- He knew how to administrate.
- He knew how to make plans.
- He knew how to set up a budget.
- He knew how to delegate.
- He knew how to communicate.

• He had mastered his gift.

Joseph had skill sets. He had numerous skills.

Dreamer, you have to develop multiple skill sets for the dream God has given you. All of the skills Joseph had, you must develop if you truly desire to fulfill your dream. Do not only learn how to use a hammer because everything is not a nail, also learn other useful tools.

There are numerous resources available to help you learn the skills you need to run an organization. Two places I highly recommend are the public library and YouTube.com. The information is free and there is a lot of it. Yes, you may come across a book or video that will not help you, but there will be plenty of information that will help you move in the right direction.

Here are some authors and speakers to look for to get you started:
1. Myles Munroe
2. Dave Ramsey
3. Michael Gerber
4. Ram Charan
5. Peter Drucker
6. John Maxwell
7. Robert Kiyosaki

Become an Asset

Joseph's business plan made sense to Pharaoh and his servants. *"The advice was good"* in their eyes (v. 37). Pharaoh turned to Joseph and said,

"Inasmuch as God has shown you all this, there is no one as discerning and wise as you. You shall be over my house, and all my people shall be ruled according to your word; only in regard to the throne will I be greater than you." Then Pharaoh said to Joseph, *"See, I have set you over all the land of Egypt."* (v.39-41)

He put Joseph over his house, the palace, and all the people, the nation of Egypt. Joseph became the second highest official in Egypt. He received the title Vizier. This is equivalent to being a Prime Minister. Joseph ran the nation of Egypt.

Joseph got the job. He was able to do what others could not do. Joseph became valuable to Pharaoh. He was an asset. Seek to become an asset, not a liability. Learn how to make positive changes to your client's (or organization's) situations and you will be an asset.

Pharaoh gave Joseph his signet ring, new royal clothes and a gold chain. These items signified authority, power, influence, and wealth. Then Joseph was given a chariot and a wife. Joseph's life has completely changed, all because he waited on God and he was ready when God brought an opportunity before him.

The 13 years of ups and downs, promotions and demotions were there to prepare him for the moment he met Pharaoh at God's appointed time. In verses 47 – 49, we find out that Joseph was not a con-artist. Not only did he have a plan, he also knew how to work the plan.

Now, in the seven plentiful years, the ground brought forth abundantly. So he gathered up all the food of the seven years, which were in the land of Egypt, and laid up the food in the cities; he laid up in every city the food of the fields which surrounded them. Joseph gathered very much grain, as the sand of the sea, until he stopped counting, for it was immeasurable. (v.59)

Dealing with the Past

During those years of plenty, Joseph and his wife had two sons. They named them Manasseh and Ephraim. We are told in Genesis 41:51, "*Joseph called the name of the firstborn Manasseh: For God has made me forget all my toil and all my father's house.*"

Not that he forgot his hardship and family back in Canaan, he was not bitter and he did not hold a grudge over what happened to him. God had helped him to see his past experience through the lens of God's grace and providence.

Then Genesis 41:52 reads, *"And the name of the second he called Ephraim: For God has caused me to be fruitful in the land of my affliction."*

God has blessed him in the very place he had all of his struggles.

What good is it for God to bless you materially and for you to advance towards your dream if you are bitter about your past? Being externally prosperous and internally bitter is not a good combination. You end up miserable and angry because of what has happened to you.

You need God to heal your heart over your past. You must deal with your bitter emotions about your hardship. Those difficult situations were preparation. Those negative people were preparation. God was using them to prepare you, not to destroy you. The blessing of reaching your dream is great but your heart being healed over your past is extremely important.

Increasing Resources

When the famine came, it hit hard. The famine hit all the nations around Egypt. For a while, the people in Egypt had food while the other nations did not. When the people in Egypt ran out of food, they *"cried out to Pharaoh for bread"* (v.55). Pharaoh told them to go and talk to Joseph and do whatever he told them to do.

The Bible say, Joseph *"opened up the storehouses and sold to the Egyptians"* (v.56). Wait, you mean Joseph did not give the food away? I thought Joseph believed in God. You can believe in God and make a profit; it's okay. Joseph increased the finances of Egypt. He made the nation profitable.

Hey dreamer, you have to learn how to increase the capital of those you work for or those that retain your serve. Capital is not always money. Capital are the items people, departments, and organizations value. Increasing capital is about making things better, more profitable.

There are at least three types of capital. Capital can be:
• Intellectual – know-how, understanding, insight, processes
• Human – Developing people, recruiting and deploying
• Financial – lowering budgets, increase sales

and profits.

Joseph increased the capital of Egypt and fed the people of Egypt. Joseph met the needs of hungry people, therefore solving their problem too.

Points to remember:
1. First impressions are crucial.
2. Give people a sample of what you can offer.
3. Seek to become an asset, not a liability.

Coaching Exercises

1. What books do you need to read to prepare you for your dream?

_____

_____

_____

_____

2. In what ways are you actively developing the skills Joseph used above?

_____

_____

_____

_____

_____

3. How can you increase the capital of those who need your service?

_____

_____

_____

_____

_____

_____

_____

Index:
1.
www.brainyquote.com/quotes/quotes/s/sainta
ugus108487.html
2.	www.sramanamitra.com/2016/08/12/cross-border-e-commerce-in-africa-mall-for-africa-ceo-chris-folayan-part-1
3. Nelson's New Illustrated Bible Manners & Customs by Howard F. Vos. P. 49

Chapter Five

The Dream Has Arrived

~ Genesis 42 – 45 ~
*"The biggest adventure you can take is to live the life
of your dreams."(1)*
- Oprah Winfrey -

In the insightful book *Spiritual Leadership* by
Henry and Richard Blackaby, they wrote about
how Christians are using their business to glorify
God. These spiritual leaders "seek to honor God
through their personal lives as well as their
business"(2). Many of these believers are not
working in Christian organizations, but they are
using their organization to honor God by helping
people and being unashamed of the Gospel of
Jesus Christ.

For these leaders, their main objective is not
personal nor organizational success at any cost.
They are endeavoring to display their Christian
beliefs and values in the marketplace. Their
dream is not to glorify themselves, but the Lord
Jesus Christ. How will you use your dream when
it arrives?

Widespread Famine

Before we enter into the details of chapter 45, we
need to back up to discuss a few important

events.

At the end of chapter 41, we are told that the famine did not only affect Egypt but *"was severe in all lands"* (41:57). This would include the land of Canaan where Joseph was from, and where his father, brothers and extended family still lived.

Chapter 42 opens with Jacob, Joseph's father, asking his sons, *"Why do you look at one another?"* (42:1). There was no grain in Canaan, but there was grain in Egypt. Jacob told his sons to go down into Egypt and buy grain so they *"may live and not die"* (42:2).

Now Jacob had 11 sons with him, but he only sent 10 of his sons to Egypt. He made his youngest son Benjamin stay in Canaan with him. Benjamin is the son that came after Joseph. Joseph and Benjamin were full brothers. They had the same mom and dad. Their mother was Rachel; the wife Jacob loved the most.

The Bible tells us when Joseph's brothers went to Egypt, *"Joseph was governor over the land"* (42:6). He was Prime Minister, running the land of Egypt. When his brothers arrived in Egypt, it just so happened, that Joseph was at the place where they had to buy grain.

It's Here

The Bible tells us, "*Joseph's brothers came and bowed before him*" (42:6). Joseph recognized his brothers instantly, but they did not recognize him. Twenty-two years have passed. Joseph is an adult. He is 39 years old.

When Joseph recognized his brothers as they bowed before him, he remembered his dreams. In the first chapter, we found out about Joseph's dreams when he was 17 years old (ch. 37). The dreams spoke of his brothers bowing before him one day. As his brothers were before him, Joseph began to talk harshly to them.

He called them spies and said they "*have come to see the nakedness of the land*" (42:9). They came to see where the land was vulnerable for an invasion. They pleaded with Joseph, telling him they were not spies but a group of brothers from the land of Canaan.

They told him, they were 12 brothers and that their youngest brother was at home and one of their brothers "*is no more*" (42:13). They believed Joseph had died. Joseph and his brothers entered into a heated argument. Joseph told them they could not leave until their youngest brother came to Egypt. And he was still calling them spies.

Then Joseph threw his 10 brothers into jail for three days. Wait, what is going on here? I thought Joseph had grown up. I thought he was not bitter about his past. That's why he named his sons Manasseh (to forget) and Ephraim (to be fruitful).

Possible Reconciliation

Why is he going through all of this, acting like he does not know his brothers? It seems as if he is being mean and then he puts them in jail for three days. At first glance, Joseph seems to still be immature. As if, this is his time to pay his brothers back for all the wrong they did to him.

But as the story unfolds, we will see that everything that Joseph put his brothers through was to make room for reconciliation so he could be reconciled and reunited to his father and brothers. Position, wealth, and power are empty if you are lonely. The dream is a lonely place to be if you do not have meaningful relationships.

The dream God has given you is not only about blessing you. The dream is for you to be in a position of influence to help those in need and to reconcile relationships. Within chapters 42 – 44, Joseph put his brothers through a series of tests to find out the emotional condition of their minds. He was seeking to find out if they had matured. Do they feel any remorse for selling him into slavery?

After spending time studying the life of Joseph, I found out that his testing showed great wisdom. It's because anyone can say they have changed, but the situations they are placed in will reveal if they truly have changed. To some degree, people do what Joseph did to his brothers every day. I hope not to the extent that Joseph did.

But when a person breaks your trust, you do not instantly extend your trust again. I hope not anyway. You want to see how they will respond to different situation with you over time before you will be willing to extend more trust to them.

After the three days, Joseph released his brothers and told them they could return home. But he kept Simeon, their second oldest brother and told them to bring back their youngest brother, Benjamin. Joseph commanded their sacks be filled with grain and without his brothers' knowledge, he put their money back in their bags.

On their journey back home to Canaan, they realized that their money had been returned and they became extremely afraid. They asked, *"What is this God has done to us?"* (42:28). They were wondering if God was dealing with them because of what they did to Joseph.

Jeopardizing the Family

When they arrived at Canaan and told Jacob what happened, their father blamed his sons for what happened. He said, "*You have bereaved me*" (42:36). They have taken people away from him. Joseph, Simeon and now they want to take Benjamin. Jacob would not let him go.

The brothers left the conversation alone. But it came back up when they began to run out of grain to eat. Jacob told his nine sons to go and buy more grain in Egypt. I will paraphrase one of his sons response, "Judah speaks up and tells his father no, not without Benjamin. The man in Egypt said, when we come back, Benjamin must be with us."

Jacob still did not want to let Benjamin go. Here's what bothers me about Jacob, he is willing to let one of his sons (Simeon) rot in jail because he does not want Benjamin to leave.

Even worst in my opinion, he is ready to jeopardize the whole family, let everyone starve to death, because he wants to keep Benjamin home. Benjamin is not a child. He is more than likely to be in his late 20's or early 30's. Benjamin is an adult.

Your love for one child cannot be so overwhelming that you are willing to sacrifice your entire family. That kind of love is unhealthy and dangerous.

Judah tells Jacob to put Benjamin in his charge and if anything happens, he will take the blame. Jacob finally agrees. Jacob sends gifts to the governor; he does not know he is his son Joseph.

Reconnecting the Family

When the brothers arrived in Egypt, "*Joseph saw that Benjamin was with them*" (43:16). Joseph told his steward to take them to his house, and make a meal because they will all eat together with Joseph. When Joseph's brothers heard they were going to the governor's house, they became scared.

They thought they were about to be punished for the money that was placed in their bags on their first trip. They told Joseph's steward about the money and told them not to worry about it. God had blessed them and they already paid for their grain from the first trip.

The steward brought Simeon out to them. All eleven brothers were together in Joseph's house.

When Joseph entered the house, they gave Joseph the gifts and they bowed before him. The dream has arrived. The eleven stars (all of his brothers) have bowed before Joseph.

Not only did they bow once but twice, and they even laid prostrate on the floor before him. It took 22 years, but the dream has come true. God did not lie. The dream was from God.

Before they had their meal together, Joseph became overwhelmed with emotion because he was speaking with his brother Benjamin. He ran out of the room and cried. After getting his composure, he came back into the room and told the servants to serve the food.

While they were eating, Joseph sent Benjamin five times more food than the other brothers to see how they would respond. But nothing happened. No one got upset. No one became jealous or envious.

They were eating and having a good time. They still did not know that the governor was Joseph. Joseph told his steward to fill up their bags with grain and put their money back in their bags again. He told the steward to put Joseph's cup in Benjamin's bag.

The next morning, the eleven brothers left for

Canaan. While they were in route, Joseph sent his steward after them. On catching up with them, he told them, one of them stole Joseph's cup and whoever stole it would become a slave. They said no way. No one stole it.

After checking all the bags, the steward found the cup in Benjamin's bag. Scripture says, "*They tore their clothes*" (44:13). They were grieving. They could not believe this was happening. They turned around and went back to Egypt.

Sacrifice

When they arrived in Egypt, they fell before Joseph. Judah began to talk to Joseph and said an interesting statement, "*God has found out the iniquity of your servants*" (44:16). They knew they had sinned against Joseph and their father and they believed God was dealing with them for it.

Joseph told the other brothers, they could leave but Benjamin would have to stay and become a slave. Judah began to plead for Benjamin's release. He informed Joseph how they could not return home without Benjamin, because their father would die. He said, "*His life is bound up in the lad's life*" (44:30).

Judah said to Joseph, "*Let your servant remain instead of the lad as a slave to my lord*" (44:33). He wanted to take Benjamin's place. He could not allow his father to lose Benjamin.

This is a pleasant surprise; the brothers had changed in behavior. As a matter of fact, Judah had changed. Judah was the one that suggested they sell Joseph into slavery. Now he was ready to sacrifice his own life, for his brother and to prevent his father from grieving to death.

We must believe that people can change, especially people who believe in the Gospel of Jesus. The very reason we tell people about the Gospel is so they can receive salvation (change of eternal destiny) and they can become like Jesus, therefore changing their lives.

When Judah attempted to trade himself for Benjamin, Genesis 45:1 tells us, "*Joseph could not restrain himself.*" He sent everyone out of the room except his brothers. He cried and said to his brothers, "*I am Joseph; does my father still live?*"

It is here that we see that Joseph was not trying to be malicious or petty. Joseph's heart was tender. He loved his brothers. He just wanted to see if they had become honest men like they said they were. He also wanted to know if they cared for all their brothers, including Benjamin.

Back Together Again

When they heard that he was Joseph, they were speechless. He told them to come near and he told them again, "*I am Joseph your brother, whom you sold into Egypt*" (45:4). The family secret has been let out of the bag.

There can be no reconciliation until the truth is told. If you want to see a broken relationship begin the process of reconciliation, be mature enough to be honest about what happened. Do not lie and attempt to cover up the problem, come clean.

Joseph told them, "*Do not therefore be grieved or angry with yourselves because you sold me here; for God sent me before you to preserve life.*" (45:5). Joseph wanted them to know that they did him wrong, but he did not want them to beat themselves up about it. God stepped in and He was the one who really sent Joseph to Egypt.

God wanted Joseph there to save people's lives, including his family in Canaan. Joseph had forgiven his brothers and he had a divine perspective on his life. His brothers did not want him around, but God wanted him in Egypt so when they came for food, Joseph would be there to feed them.

Understand, if folks had not sold you out, you would not be as strong as you are today. If they had not abandoned you, you would not know God like you know Him now. Stop holding a grudge. Forgive them and if possible, reconcile with them.

Author Philip Yancey writes, "Christian faith is... basically about love and being loved and reconciliation. These things are so important, they're foundational and they can transform individuals, families."(3)

God may have sent you before them, so you can learn how to trust God and for you to grow up. Therefore, when they need help, you can be there for them.

The Dream is Bigger than You

The dream God gave Joseph was bigger than his brothers bowing to him. Your dream is bigger than people respecting you and looking up to you. The dream has been given to you so God can use you to help save lives and to help bring about the process of reconciliation.

People everywhere need to be reconciled to God and in order for that to happen, usually someone who they respect will need to talk to them about

Jesus. Someone with influence has to have a conversation with them about the Gospel. The dream is to help you have influence so you can help people for the glory of God.

Not only do people need to be reconciled to God, people need to be reconciled to one another. Marriages need to be restored, but couples will need to talk to someone they respect who has a healthy marriage. Broken families need to be restored, but those families will need to talk to someone who has lived out the dream of restoring their family.

The dream is bigger than people applauding you. Achieving the dream means you can help people receive reconciliation. People are hurting and broken. They need someone who they can respect and have been through some problems and still believe in Jesus to talk to them about what they are going through. They can then be pointed to the Rock of our Salvation, Jesus the Christ, so they can be reconciled to God and hopefully to other people.

When your dream arrives, how will you glorify God with it? Will you use your platform to help people and share the love and Gospel of Jesus?

Points to remember:

1. Your dream is not only about you receiving a blessing.

2. There can be no reconciliation with truth.

3. There are people in every country and industry that need to be reconciled to God.

Coaching Exercises

1. Do you know how to share the Gospel of Jesus Christ?
Learn the ABC's of the Gospel:

• <u>A</u>ccept everyone is a sinner in need of a savior. (Romans 3:23)

• <u>B</u>elieve Jesus is the Savior who shed His blood, died, was buried and resurrected for everyone's sins. (Romans 10:9)

• <u>C</u>onfess Jesus to be the Lord of their life. (Romans 10:9)

2. What is your testimony in receiving salvation? Below is how you can structure your testimony. Keep the explanation between 3 - 5 minutes.
• How was your life before Jesus?

_____
_____
_____
_____

•How did you meet Jesus? (How and when did you receive salvation?)

_____
_____
_____
_____

•How has your life changed since you have been following Jesus?

_____

_____

_____

_____

3. What has God helped you deal with and overcome while you have been a believer?

_____

_____

_____

_____

4. Will you be courageous to share the Gospel and your testimony with those you will encounter on the journey to your dream?

_____

Index:

1.
www.brainyquote.com/quotes/quotes/o/oprah winfr383916.html

2. Spiritual Leadership, Henry & Richard Blackaby. P. 141. B&H Publishing Group

3.
www.brainyquote.com/quotes/quotes/p/philip yanc527075.html

Chapter Six

Prospering in the Midst of the Famine

~ Genesis 46 – 47 ~
"I want to be the bridge to the next generation."(1)
- Michael Jordan -

In the United States, when someone commits a crime, receives a felony conviction and is imprisoned, and when they are released after serving their jail term, they enter a famine. They are unable to vote, and many of them are unable to get a job paying a decent wage because of their felony. Therefore, many will return to a life of crime and end up back in prison. This is known as recidivism. It's the cycle of imprisonment; release, then imprisonment again and the cycle repeats.

While there are many factors that play into the process of recidivism, there is a company in Wheaton, Illinois who is attempting to break the cycle. The name of the business is Second Chance Coffee Company. The brand name of their coffee is I Have a Bean. Their aspiration is not only to make amazing coffee, they also aspire to help felons start a new life when they leave prison. They hire individuals with felony convictions to work in the business.

Peter Leonard, the CEO, is attempting to operate

his business for the glory of God by doing business in excellence and helping people in need in Illinois. The company's website says,

"Second Chance Coffee Company operates under the premise that we can use every part of our business to "love our neighbor as ourselves" to positively impact the spiritual, social and economic condition of our employees, their families and the communities in which they live."(2)

Second Chance Coffee Company is attempting to help people who are in a famine to prosper. They are helping to change people's lives through coffee, employment, and godly principles.

The Future Awaits

As we have studied the life of Joseph, I pray you have seen the road to your dream is not easy. The journey is filled with hardship, waiting and providential moments. You will have situations where you are in a pit (bad moments) and you will have palace experiences too (the blessing of God).

As you progress through these highs and lows, I encourage you to hold on to Jesus. Do not put much stock in your current situation, even as you attempt to make the best out of it. Do not place too much value on where you find yourself in life, because your situations can change in a moment. We have seen this in the life of Joseph and will see the changes in the lives of Joseph's family, Pharaoh, and the Egyptians.

After Joseph and his brothers reconciled in chapter 45, Joseph and Pharaoh told Joseph's brothers to go back to Canaan and get Jacob and their families and come to Egypt to live. Pharaoh gave them moving supplies in order to bring their families to Egypt. From Canaan to Egypt was about a three-week journey (between 250 – 300 miles) during that time.

Joseph sent them back with twenty donkeys loaded with food for their journey back to Canaan. We are seeing God prosper Israel (Jacob and his descendants) in the midst of the famine. But in order for their prosperity to continue, they must transition themselves from Canaan to Egypt. They must leave the familiar and comfortable and move into the unknown and uncomfortable (which was discussed in a previous chapter).

Taking a Risk

In order for us to see the continual provision of God, we must move from the familiar to the unknown. This will require us to walk by faith and not by sight. This will be uncomfortable at times, but it will be needed to see the mighty hand of God at work in our lives. You must develop your faith to follow your dream.

When Joseph's brothers arrived home, Canaan, they told Jacob that Joseph was alive and he was the governor of Egypt. The scripture says, *"Jacob's heart stood still"* (45:26). Jacob almost had a heart attack *"because he did not believe them"* (45:26). When Jacob saw everything that Joseph sent, he accepted that Joseph was alive.

In chapter 46, Jacob and his family traveled to Egypt from Canaan. We are told that on their way to Egypt, Jacob stopped at Beer-sheba to offer *"sacrifices to God"* (46:1). God reassured Jacob through dreams that Egypt was where they were supposed to be.

One way to help develop your faith is to spend time in prayer. As you spend time talking with God, He will give you the assurance you need to a take risk and to follow His guidance. How is your prayer life?

God also informed Jacob it would be in Egypt that God would make him a great nation. But, God would also bring them out of Egypt since Egypt was not the final destination for the people of Israel.

It is here we begin to see the book of Exodus come into focus, which shows us that God always keeps His word. In Exodus, we are told how God brought the nation of Israel out of Egypt by the mighty hand of God.

In verses 8 – 27 of chapter 46, Moses gives us the names of the individual family members who migrate into Egypt. We are told that there were 70 people who transitioned into Egypt to live.

Moment of a Lifetime

When Jacob's family arrived in Egypt, Joseph met them in the land of Goshen, which was on the eastern border of Egypt, near the Nile River. It was the most fertile land in Egypt. It was the best land in the nation. It was great for shepherding flocks.

When Joseph saw Jacob, it was an emotional experience. The Bible tells us, Joseph "*fell on his [Jacob] neck and wept on his neck a good while*" (46:29). This was a time of long hugs and a lot of tears. After 22 years of separation, a family reunion occurred. For a long time, Joseph did not know if his father was alive, that is why he asked his brothers "*does my father still live?*" (45:3).

After their reunion, Joseph began to prep Jacob

and his brothers for their meeting with Pharaoh. Joseph told them, he would go to Pharaoh and let him know that his relatives had arrived. He would also inform Pharaoh that they were shepherds and they had their folks and herds with them.

Mentoring

Then Joseph told them, *"when Pharaoh calls you, he will ask, what is your occupation?"* (46:33). Basically, Pharaoh values work and skilled labor. You say, *"Your servants' occupation has been with livestock from our youth even till now, both we and our fathers"* (46:34). He told them this so they will be able to live in Goshen.

Then Joseph makes an interesting statement at the end of the verse 34, he said, *"For every shepherd is an abomination to the Egyptians."* Let me show you what Joseph did for his father and brothers. He gave them a crash course in royal court etiquette and Egyptian culture.

When we go to see Pharaoh:
1. Wait for him to call you. Do not just walk up to him.
2. When he asks you a question, respect his position, say, "Your servants are shepherds."
3. Tell the truth. Tell him you are shepherds.
4. Understand, the Egyptians do not like you.

They are given to prejudice. They believe your occupation is an abomination.

Basically, the culture is against you and how you live. Joseph wanted them to understand this before they made a life in Egypt. He told them what they would be facing in their new environment.

When God allows you to make it to your dream, do not forget those who are coming after you, especially those who want your advice and guidance. Do not make them experience the mistakes that could have easily been avoided if you would have helped them see the landscape of their new environment. It is a sad fact of life that there are many people who do not want to help the next generation.

That is why I believe many people are stuck today because the previous generation did not want to help the upcoming generation. Therefore, each generation of people have to start from scratch. Many mistakes could have been avoided if the previous generation had shared their experience and know-how with the new generation.

I am not only talking about culturally, but also in the marketplace and in the church. Senior managers should guide new managers. Pastors must teach new ministers about the different facets of ministry. Veterans at the shops should help new folks on the floor. Do not forget to share your wisdom and know-how with those coming behind you, especially with those who are asking for your assistance.

Open the Door

In the beginning of chapter 47, Joseph took five of his brothers to go and see Pharaoh. We do not know why he chose five but he did. When they met Pharaoh, he asked them exactly what Joseph said he was going to ask. *"What is your occupation?"* (47:3).

They told Pharaoh they were shepherds and they were there because Canaan had been hit hard by the famine. Therefore, they were unable to pasture their flocks there anymore. Then they asked, *"Please let your servants dwell in the land of Goshen?"* (47:4).

I really appreciate the fact that they made a case for themselves. Even though Joseph coached them, they explained their own situation. You do not have to become mimics of your mentors but you should learn all that you can from them. They spoke for themselves and they asked for what was offered to them.

They did not become greedy and ask for more because their brother was a big shot in Egypt. They basically said, we do not need anything extra from you, just allow us to live on the land and we will take care of ourselves. When someone opens a door for you using their capital (political, corporate, relational), do not abuse their generosity and help.

You do not need extra privileges, all you need is a shot. All you need is the door to be opened, the opportunity. If you know your stuff, know your craft, know how to be a good shepherd and with the mighty hand of God on your side, you will be able to take care of yourself. The pasture in Egypt may be different than Canaan, but if you know your craft, you will be able to figure it out.

Pharaoh told Joseph, *"Have your father and brothers live in the best land, the land of Goshen"* (47:6). Then he suggested, *"If you know any competent men among them, then make them chief herdsmen over my livestock"* (47:6). Pharaoh offered Joseph's brothers supervisory jobs in the government based off of Joseph's recommendation. Those competent shepherds would be able to supervise the Egyptian cattlemen.

God continued to open doors for them since they had reconciled with their bother Joseph. After the brothers met with Pharaoh, Joseph brought Jacob in to meet Pharaoh. Jacob blessed Pharaoh at the beginning and at the end of their conversation. Joseph situated his father and brothers in the best part of Egypt and gave them food to eat.

God has blessed them. God is prospering them. While God is blessing Joseph's family, Moses reminds us that the famine is still occurring. But, Joseph's family was being blessed because they were where they were supposed to be and they were learning from someone that went before them.

Not only should you mentor those that come behind you, but also you must be willing to learn from those who have gone before you. Are you willing to learn from your predecessor? Their wisdom will help guide you into the blessings God has waiting for you.

Thinking Outside the Box

The famine was so severe that the Egyptians ran out of money. They spent all their money buying food from Joseph. The scripture tells us, "*Joseph gathered up all the money*" and "*brought the money into Pharaoh's house*" (47:14). Joseph was increasing the financial position of the nation, giving Egypt a better cash position.

When the Egyptians' money ran out, Joseph set up a bartering system. Joseph was thinking creatively. The Egyptians exchanged their livestock for food. Joseph was increasing the nation's assets. Pharaoh already owned livestock, but because of Joseph, Pharaoh's livestock assets were increasing.

Pharaoh was now prospering in the midst of the famine because of Joseph's wise business practice. Joseph was not ripping people off. People had a need and God put Joseph in a place to fill their need.

As a dreamer, you must learn how to think outside of the box. You have to be someone who thinks creatively. One way to learn how to do this is to find out how other people or organizations in your field are operating and learn from them. It will help you to look at problems and solutions from different angles.

Remember the Past

The next year, the Egyptians came back to Joseph and told him they have no money and no more cattle. All they have is their land and themselves. The Egyptians offer to sell themselves and their land to Pharaoh for seed so they would not die and for their land not to become desolate. The Egyptians care about themselves and the land of

Egypt.

We must understand that Joseph did not ask them to sell themselves or their lands. They offered. He did ask for their money and their livestock but not for their lives and lands. Look at the difficult situation Joseph is put in.

Joseph knows the experience of slavery and bondage; but, however, he cannot give the grain away. It is not his to give. It's Pharaoh's grain. Look at Joseph's wisdom.

He bought all the land for Pharaoh. Every Egyptian that had land, sold it to Joseph. Joseph moved all the Egyptians off of the land they sold and put them into the cities. Do you remember where the grain was stored? In the cities. He moved them closer to the food supply. The only land he did not touch was the land owned by the Egyptian priests.

The wise actions of Joseph square with Egyptian history. History lets us know that under the reign of Sesostris III, he "effectively reduced the power of the nomarchs and brought them and the land in general under control of the crown."(3) Many historians point to Sesostris III as the one who consolidated power and land. The Bible lets everyone know it was Joseph who worked out the deal with the Egyptians.

Everyone Benefits

The agreement Joseph constructed between Pharaoh and the Egyptians is very creative. When the famine ended, Joseph told the Egyptians, *"I bought you and your land this day for Pharaoh."* He said, *"Here is seed for you to sow the land"* (47:23). When the harvest comes, one-fifth (20%) goes to Pharaoh and the other four-fifth (80%) you can keep to feed yourselves and your families.

Joseph allows them to move back to their homes and they can work the land. The Egyptians are allowed to keep 80% of the harvest for themselves. They basically become tenant farmers. They do not own the land but they can benefit from the land. They worked on Pharaoh's land and paid him a portion of the crop so they can live there and live off the land.

Now, you could be thinking, "Oh my, I cannot believe Joseph took that deal and made those people slaves and only gave them 80%." Well, he could have given them 20% and Pharaoh 80%. Or he could have taken all of the harvest and rationed out small daily portions. But he did not do that. Joseph kept their dignity intact and they thanked him for it. They said, *"You have saved our lives"* (47:25).

What can we learn from this? When you are in a position of power, do not take advantage of people. Do not exploit their vulnerabilities and weakness when they are in need. Be fair. Leave people's dignity intact. Do not abuse them; help them, and bless them. Honor God in the way you treat them

Also, remember where you came from. Remember how you felt and how you were treated when you began at the company and had no influence, or when you began your business. Remember and do right towards people because you are representing God there.

The Best Mentors

While I was thinking about this chapter, I came across a provocative article on Harvard Business Review website (hbr.org) by Anthony K. Tjan. He is an author and the CEO of the venture capital firm Cue Ball. The article is titled, "What the Best Mentors Do"(4).

In the article, Mr. Tjan writes what he has learned about mentoring after interviewing numerous leaders. He boiled his learning down to four behaviors. Joseph also demonstrated these four behaviors while he mentored his brothers.

The first behavior is, "Put the relationship before

the mentorship." Tjan writes about how mentoring can become more of an item on a to-do list than an authentic relationship. The better mentoring dynamic includes rapport and chemistry, and the mentor and the mentee must have found "common ground as people."

When we look at Joseph mentoring his brothers before they stood before Pharaoh, we see he and his brother had an authentic relationship. Joseph did not help his brother out of obligation. He mentored them because he cared for them.

The next behavior is, "Focus on character rather than competency." The article speaks to character as "soft matters." These "soft matters" or soft skills are important. The best mentors help the mentees to understand that character is crucial, that soft skills matter.

Joseph understood soft skills mattered. He emphasized with his brothers to tell the truth. When Pharaoh asked them their occupation, they were not supposed to lie. He knew the Egyptians didn't like shepherds, but they disliked liars even more. Joseph understood that character is crucial and that soft skills matter.

The third behavior is, "Shout loudly with your optimism, and keep quiet with your cynicism." Tjan wrote, "Mentors need to be givers of energy, not takers of it." Good mentors should encourage their mentees to explore their ideas and opportunities. The mentor's job is not only to help their mentee to think more realistic but also to encourage them to see possibilities.

No time while Joseph was mentoring his brothers do we find Joseph telling his brothers what they were doing wrong. The way he mentored them was full of optimism and encouragement. Joseph's mentoring style helped his brothers to see possibilities not roadblocks.

The final behavior is, "Be more loyal to your mentee than you are to your company." I agree with Anthony Tjan when he wrote, "the best mentors recognize ... the best way to inspire commitment is to be fully and selflessly committed to the best interests of colleagues and employees." In a mentoring relationship, the mentors should focus on what's best for the mentee first, then what's best for the company. Help the mentee find their passion and calling even if that road leads the mentee outside of the organization.

Joseph demonstrated this skill too. He was loyal to Pharaoh and Egypt, but he put his family first. He showed them how to navigate Egypt's royal court and politics. Joseph was not attempting to do harm to Egypt, he was attempting to help his brothers get the best possible outcome for their lives and families. Joseph was more loyal to his mentees than his company, Egypt.

We can learn to become better mentors from the example of Joseph and the wisdom of Mr. Tjan.

Points to remember:
1. Do not forget to help the next generation.
2. You do not need extra privileges; all you need is an opportunity.
3. Honor God in how you treat people.

Coaching Exercises

1. Who are you mentoring?

_____

_____

_____

2. Who are your mentors?

_____

_____

_____

If there are no mentors available, read books, listen to podcasts, watch videos, go to conference in the area of your dream.

3. Which people/organizations can you learn from to help you think more creatively?

_____

_____

_____

Index:

1.
www.brainyquote.com/quotes/quotes/m/mich
aeljor447186.html
2. www.ihaveabean.com
3. Nelson's New Illustrated Bible Manners &
Customs by Howard F. Vos. P. 50
4. www.hbr.org/2017/02/what-the-best-
mentors-do

Chapter Seven

The Legacy of the Dreamer

~ Genesis 47 – 50 ~
"If you want to change the world, go home and love your family."(1)
- Mother Teresa -

An Albanian grocer named Nikola Bojaxhiu and his wife Dranafile had their third child. The date is August 26, 1910 in city of Skopje, which is known today as Macedonia. Their third baby was a girl. This precious girl grew up and among other things, she won the Nobel Peace Prize in 1979. But instead of having the Nobel banquet honoring her achievements, she requested that the entire budget of the banquet be used to help the poor. The budget was $192,000.

Who is this amazingly selfless woman? Her name is Agnes Gonxha Bojaxhiu. You may know her by the name she chose at the age of 18 when she became a Catholic nun in 1931, Mother Teresa. After 15 years of being in the nunnery, Sisters of Loretto, and teaching at St. Mary's high school in Calcutta, India, she received her "call within her call." She became aware of the people she was called to serve, the poorest of poor.

Mother Teresa left the order of the Sisters of Loretto and moved into the slums of Calcutta to serve them. She did not have any money or resources but she had passion to help "the least of these" (Matthew 25:40). It has been said, that when she began to teach the poverty-stricken children of Calcutta how to read, she would use a stick and write the information in the dirt.

Mother Teresa's journey in helping the poor, orphans, and the ill was not easy. There were times when she had dark moments, when she felt as if God was silent. Yet, she continued to emphasize God's tender love while she helped those in need. In 1950, Mother Teresa established Missionaries of Charity. Overtime, the order has grown past 4000 nuns and 400 brothers and reaching into over 100 countries.

Mother Teresa has won numerous awards for her service, the Indian Padma Shri (1962), the Peace Prize (1971), the Nobel Peace Prize (1979), and the Albanian Golden Honor of the Nation (1994). Mother Teresa died on September 5, 1997 and left behind a legacy of love, compassion, sacrifice and leadership.

Legacy

We have reached the end of our journey as we look at the life of Joseph, the dreamer. I pray this study has helped you to see the dream God has given you with more clarity. And you understand that the dream is bigger than you, so God can be glorified in the earth, and people can move from death to life by receiving Jesus as their Savior.

In this last chapter, we will look at Joseph's legacy. Your legacy is what you leave behind for the next generation. When you die, what will be your legacy? How will you be remembered? What impression will you leave on the world?

While some people may say that Joseph's legacy was his administrative skills and his governmental prowess. He was able to save Egypt and the surrounding nations from starvation. In the process he helped Egypt become a more powerful empire. Yes, Joseph and the gracious hand of God did all this.

While some people would stop there at Joseph's external achievements, wealth, power and influence, I would say that is only part of his legacy. As a matter of fact, if your legacy stops at the external trimmings of life, you have a pretty shallow legacy.

I believe it is a good thing to leave behind a statement of the importance of work, achievement and accomplishments. But I do not only want to be remembered, as being a hard worker. Joseph's legacy had more depth than his dream. From the end of chapter 47 through the end of chapter 50, we see the other half of Joseph's legacy.

Do Not Neglect Your Family

When the famine had come to its conclusion in chapter 47 and verses 27 – 31, we are told that the people of Israel were multiplying within Egypt. Joseph's father, Jacob, was coming to the end of his life and Jacob asked Joseph to handle his funeral arrangements.

So Israel dwelt in the land of Egypt, in the country of Goshen; and they had possessions there and grew and multiplied exceedingly. And Jacob lived in the land of Egypt seventeen years. So the length of Jacob's life was one hundred and forty-seven years. When the time drew near that Israel must die, he called his son Joseph and said to him, "Now if I have found favor in your sight, please put your hand under my thigh, and deal kindly and truly with me. Please do not bury me in Egypt, but let me lie with my fathers; you shall carry me out of Egypt and bury me in their burial place." And he said, "I will do as you have said." Then he said, "Swear to me." And he swore to him. So Israel bowed himself on the head of the bed. (Ch. 47:27-31)

Jacob wanted to be buried back in the land of Canaan. Jacob asked Joseph to promise to bury him in Canaan and Joseph agreed.

Within these verses and the next few chapters, we are able to see with much clarity, what is truly important to Joseph. It's his immediate and external family. Joseph was at the bedside of his father, seeing to his concerns and wishes. He was not off trying to conquer the next accomplishment.

Instead, he was taking time out of his busy schedule to talk with and spend time with his aging father. When it is all said and done, you do not want to have regrets of not spending time with your loved ones before they die. Yes, you have to work and I understand you may be busy. But, one of the worst feelings you will have to live with is the regret of not spending time with those you love.

The world will not fall apart if you take a day off to see about a sick family member, or take an afternoon or morning to spend time with an aging parent or grandparent. Walt Disney puts it like this, "A man should never neglect his family for business."(2)

Spiritual Heritage

In chapter 48, Joseph came back to see Jacob again. Joseph was told that his father was really sick, so he went to see him. But, this time, he brought his two sons with him, Manasseh and Ephraim. When Joseph and his sons entered the house, the Bible tells us, *"Israel strengthened himself and sat up on the bed"* (48:2).

We have three generations in the room, Jacob, Joseph and Joseph's sons. Jacob told Joseph, while Joseph's sons were there, about his life. He told him of his encounter with God at Luz (Bethel) (Genesis 35:6 – 12), where God told Jacob, He was going to multiply the children of Jacob and God was going to give Jacob's descendants the land of Canaan.

Joseph was able to hear a portion of his father's life that he had never heard, all because he made himself available to spend time with his dying father. He and his sons were able to learn about their spiritual heritage because they made time for family.

Does your family know their spiritual heritage? Do your children and grandchildren know how you got saved, when you gave your life to Jesus? Do they know how God has changed your life and fulfilled the promises He gave you? If they do not, you are doing them a grave injustice by keeping their spiritual heritage away from them.

When you read further into chapter 48, you find out that Jacob adopted Joseph's sons and they received a portion of Jacob's inheritance and the land of Canaan. Then Jacob laid his hands on Joseph's sons and blessed them.

The Blessings

What I find interesting is, while Jacob was blessing Manasseh and Ephraim, *"he blessed Joseph"* too (48:15). But, I thought he was blessing Joseph's sons. He was blessing them and Joseph at the same time, which leads me to conclude that, when my kids are blessed, I am blessed in the process too.

I have two sons, Stephen Jr. and Rasheed, and when they are doing well and are safe, I feel blessed. When my children are being blessed and moving forward in life, because I am their father, I should feel blessed too. Not that I am directly receiving the blessing, but because God is blessing them, I am being indirectly blessed. When your children are being blessed, you should feel blessed too.

It is crazy to see parents competing with their children. That is foolishness. You should want your children to do better than you and go farther than you in life. Be excited about their future because it is connected to your future.

Jacob also blessed Joseph with a double portion

of land. He received *"one portion above his brothers"* (48:22). Joseph received the blessing of the first-born son. We see Jacob leaving an inheritance to his son and grandsons. As Proverbs 13:22 tells us, *"A good man leaves an inheritance to his children's children."*

Clear the Air

In chapter 49, Jacob called all 12 of his sons around his bedside; one final family meeting before their father would die. Jacob told his sons about their lives and future. He told them about their character and conduct. He began with the oldest Reuben and ended with the youngest Benjamin.

Jacob spent most of his time addressing Judah and Joseph, both of which became very prominent and powerful tribes within the nation of Israel. But, here is what I would like for you to see. Joseph is there with his brothers. He does not get his time and then the brothers get their time. No, they are all there together spending time with their father before he passes away.

Do not let the sins and wrongs of the past keep you away from spending time with your family. Joseph had truly moved on with his life. He wanted to be with his family during the last days of his father's life.

It is sad to say but we can see the worst behavior out of people during funerals. You can see siblings not wanting to be in the same room while their parents are sick or dying. I just want to tell them, "Get over it, it's not about you. This moment is about the person laying on the sickbed."

Making Preparations

After Jacob had blessed all of his sons, he told them he wanted to be buried in Canaan. Jacob had finally done some parenting that I am encouraged by. Back in chapter 47, Jacob told Joseph he wanted to be buried in Canaan.

Now in chapter 48, he told the whole family where he would like to be buried, that is Canaan. Jacob removed all of the arguments out of the funeral arrangements. His children did not have to fight over what they believed their father wanted since their father had told all of them his wishes. Jacob was allowing his children to mourn his death properly.

I am not attempting to be morbid. Yet, if you are an elderly parent, make sure all your children know what you want before you pass on. By all means, have a will. At the very least, go to a department store and purchase a fill-in-the-blank will.

It does not matter what you have, someone in your family will want it. Get over your fear of people being mad at your decision. It is your stuff; you can do what you want with it. That way, your family will not be fighting over your items when you are gone.

After Jacob told everyone his last will and testament, he laid down and *"breathed his last"* while his family was around him. Joseph fell on Jacob's face weeping and kissed him goodbye. Joseph was able to spend the last 17 years of Jacob's life with his dad. Joseph made the most of every moment.

Joseph and his family took Jacob to Canaan to bury him as requested. Not only did Jacob's family go to Canaan for the funeral, so did a host of Egyptians. There were so many Egyptians at the funeral, that the Canaanites thought it was an Egyptian funeral.

Do Not Fear

After the funeral, when everyone was back in Egypt, Joseph's brothers became afraid of Joseph. They assumed that with their father being dead, they were open for Joseph to take vengeance on them. They said, what if he *"repay us for all the evil which we did to him?"* (50:1).

They sent a message to Joseph, saying, that their father wanted them to ask Joseph to forgive them for doing him wrong 39 years ago. When Joseph heard the message, he wept. They did not understand Joseph at all. Joseph had moved on with his life. He had forgiven them already.

Their problem was they could not let go of the past. They were looking at Joseph through the lens of what they would do if they were in his position, instead of looking at Joseph for who he was and what he had done for them over the past 17 years while they were in Egypt. Joseph called his brothers to him and when they arrived, they fell before him and said, *"We are your servants"* (50:18).

In verses 19 – 21, we see Joseph's theological understanding of God.

Joseph said, *"Do not be afraid, for am I in the place of God? But as for you, you meant evil against me; but God meant it for good, in order to bring it about as it is this day, to save many people alive. Now therefore, do not be afraid; I will provide for you and your little ones." And he comforted them and spoke kindly to them.*

He reassured them, letting them know they had

nothing to fear from him. When Joseph asked, "*if he was in the place of God,*" it shows us Joseph knew his role in the family's reconciliation process.

Joseph's role is not to take revenge; he is to forgive. For him to take revenge against his brothers is to punish them as if he were God. Joseph knew he was not God. Vengeance is the role of God, not people. God said, "*Vengeance is mine, and I will repay*" (Romans 12:19). Coretta Scott King has a great statement about revenge. She said, "Revenge and retaliation always perpetuate the cycle of anger, fear and violence."(3)

Let us not attempt to avenge ourselves; we should leave that into the hands of God. When we avenge ourselves, we cause more pain, problems, and destruction. The vengeance of God corrects, builds, and transforms lives. When people try and take revenge against others, they are stepping into the place of God and humans always make horrible gods.

God is in Control

Joseph continued and told them, "*You meant evil against me, but God meant it for good, in order to bring it about as it is this day, to save many lives*" (50:20). Yes, you did me wrong brothers, but your plans were overruled by the plan of God. I am not excusing your actions but God had a bigger purpose in mind for what I went through.

The Apostle Paul would say it like this in Romans 8:29:

"We know that all things work together for good to those who love God, to those who are the called according to His purpose."

No matter what you go through, if you love God and have salvation (are the called according to His purpose), everything works for your good. I do not know how it will work for your good but it will ultimately work for your good. We do not need to know how it will work because we know the Who (God) that will make it work.

Joseph assured them again, *"Do not be afraid"* (50:19). Then he promised, *"I will provide for you and your little ones"* (50:21). They were looking to be his servants but he said, 'No, I'm going to be your provider. This is not a lord-servant relationship. We are brothers. We are family. I will be there for you and your family.'

Impacting Future Generations

The other side of Joseph's legacy was the love he showed to his family and his example of forgiveness and reconciliation. Joseph grew old in peace with his children, grand children and his extended family around him. At the end of Joseph's life, he was not talking about his great exploits and his dreams; he was spending time with his family.

You see him loving and caring for his family and extended family. He is pouring love into future generations. He is pouring love economically, emotionally and spiritually.

Joseph told his extended family in Genesis 50:24, *"God will surely visit you, and bring you out of this land to the land He swore to Abraham, to Isaac and to Jacob."* In verse 25, he instructed them to carry his bones out of Egypt when leaving. He reminded them of their spiritual heritage and God's promise for their lives.

Do you know what happened 400 years later? God visited them and raised up a man named Moses, the same man that wrote the book of Genesis. God used him to bring the people of Israel out of Egypt. When they left, Moses took Joseph's bones with them (Exodus 13:19). Then when Joshua led Israel after Moses and they conquered most of Canaan, Joshua buried Joseph's bones in Shechem in Canaan (Joshua 24:32).

Joseph's legacy left such an impression on the nation of Israel, that they carried Joseph's bones for over 40 years. How will your legacy affect your family, the family of God, and Egypt (people who do not know Jesus)? I pray it will be for good, to save lives and to bring reconciliation.

Points to remember:
1. Be remembered for something other than being a hard worker.
2. At the end of your life, what is truly important is family.
3. Tell your family their spiritual heritage.

Coaching Exercises

1. Who have you neglected to spend time with?

_____
_____
_____

2. How do you want to be remembered?

_____
_____
_____
_____
_____
_____

3. What inheritance will you leave for your family?
•
Spiritual:_____

_____
_____

• Relational:

_____
_____

• Financial:

_____
_____

Index:

1. www.azquotes.com/quote/879661
2.
www.brainyquote.com/quotes/quotes/w/waltd
isney131654.html
3.
www.brainyquote.com/quotes/quotes/c/corett
asco810107.html

CONCLUSION

"By faith Joseph, when he was dying, made mention of the departure of the children of Israel, and gave instructions concerning his bones."
~ Hebrews 11:22 ~

When we turn to the New Testament, we find the church of Jesus still talking about Joseph. The author of the book of Hebrew listed him among the heroes of the faith. When God inspires the Hebrew writer to mention Joseph, God did not want us to remember Joseph for his great exploits and political genius. God wanted us to remember Joseph for his faith.

When Joseph was on his deathbed, he was still looking to the future. He was sharing another dream—how God was going to bring the nation of Israel out of Egypt. He wanted to make sure he was a part of it when it happened, even if it was only his bones. He desired to be a part of what God was going to do.

If God was to move on someone to write about your life in one sentence, how would they describe your life? Would that sentence declare to the world and future generations that you were a person of faith? That even on your deathbed, you were dreaming and declaring what God was going to do in the future? When it's all said and done, I hope you will be remembered as a faith-filled dreamer.

About the Author

Stephen Owens is a pastor and author. He is the pastor at Mt. Calvary Baptist Church in Bedford, Ohio. Before becoming the pastor of Mt. Calvary, Stephen planted Triumphant Assembly — A CHURCH FOR THOSE THAT WANT MORE OUT OF LIFE. Stephen has over 20 years of ministry experience, which ranges from Sunday school teacher to pastor. Stephen has a passion for encouraging leaders to be all that God wants them to be. Whether they are in the marketplace or in the church, Stephen has an encouraging word for them.

Sign up for the **Leading Well Newsletter** and receive a FREE Ebook – **Rescuing Ambition.** Go here: www.Bit.ly/LeadWellNewsletter.

<u>LEAVE A REVIEW:</u>
If this book is helpful to you PLEASE leave a positive review on Amazon. Thank you.
Go here: www.amazon.com/Stephen-Owens

How to contact Stephen:
Email: s.owens.enterprises@gmail.com
Website: www.stephenowens.org &
 www.mtcalvaryofbedford.org

LinkedIn: linkedin.com/in/stephenowens1
Facebook: facebook.com/DevelopingLeadership
Twitter: twitter.com/Owens_Ministry
Instagram: instagram.com/sospeaker

Coaching with Stephen Owens

Sign up to receive three **FREE** video coaching sessions with Stephen Owens. These sessions will take you deeper into the principles and coaching exercises within Dream Chasers. Do not miss this great opportunity to develop the needed skills to purse your God given dream. Go here: www.stephenowens.org/dreamchasersbook.

Other Books by Stephen Owens

Are you looking for more encouragement as you purse your dream? If so, sign up for The Leading Well Newsletter and you will receive a FREE e-book entitled, Rescuing Ambition. Sign up TODAY at www.stephenowens.org

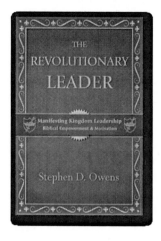

In The Revolutionary Leader you will learn how the role of leadership has been transformed. If you are a part of the Kingdom of God you are poised to unlock your leadership potential. Within the Kingdom of God, leadership is not only for the elite. It is available to every born again believer. In The Revolutionary Leader you will learn the essential components needed to become an effective leader for the glory of God. Order your copy TODAY at www.stephenowens.org.

Leading within the local church context is rewarding yet difficult. It requires constant focus on the Lord while making disciples who will follow Him with their whole heart. Those that want to lead well will have to sacrifice their time,

energy, and comfort. But, the eternal reward will surpass everything that has been sacrificed. In "Lead!" you will discover nine principles the Apostle Paul used during his apostolic career as he planted churches that lead people to Christ. Order your copy TODAY at www.stephenowens.org.

CPSIA information can be obtained
at www.ICGtesting.com
Printed in the USA
LVOW10s1337030518
575850LV00027B/239/P